Fishing Central California

A No Nonsense Guide to Spin, Bait, and Fly Fishing

Brian Milne

Guide Guy Jeans points out a rising rainbow to an angler on the North Fork of the Kern River.

NO NONSENSE

Fishing Central California
A No Nonsense Guide to Spin, Bait, and
Fly Fishing

ISBN-10: 1-892469-18-9
ISBN-13: 978-1-892469-18-2

© 2007 Brian Milne

Published by:
No Nonsense Fly Fishing Guidebooks
P.O. Box 91858
Tucson, AZ 85752-1858
(520) 547-2462
www.nononsenseguides.com

1 2 3 4 5   10 09 08 07

Printed in China

Editor: Howard Fisher
Maps, Photographs: Brian Milne
Design & Production: Doug Goewey;
              Pete Chadwell, Dynamic Arts

About the Cover

Front—John White fishing for
largemouth bass at Santa Margarita Lake
(top left), rockcod off the Monterey
coast (bottom left), fishing for surfperch
near San Simeon (bottom right).

Back—An angler fly-fishes the North
Fork of the Kern River in the fall (top).

All cover photos by Brian Milne.

The author with a nice rainbow trout.

Fish With Care

When fishing, it is extremely important to take every
necessary safety precaution prior to hitting the trail and
going out on the water. When fishing in the backcountry,
be sure to check the weather report and keep a first-aid
kit and any other necessary medical supplies on hand.

   As with any recreational activity, the proper training,
preparation, equipment and professional guidance are
recommended. To keep our favorite fisheries open to the
public, respect private property and take care of all our
natural resources.

   When fishing new waters, or for unfamiliar species,
check the rules and regulations with the California
Department of Fish and Game (www.dfg.ca.gov), as
they change often. While the information in this book
was current as of press time, changes to fees, regulations,
parks, roads, and trails do occur.

   I strongly encourage anglers to practice catch and
release and to leave the wilderness as they find it by
packing out what is packed in. Conservation and
preservation will allow us to pass on these precious
waters to future generations.

Good luck on the water,
—Brian Milne

Fishing Central California

What's inside this fishing guide

Anyone can toss a line in the water and get lucky once in a while, but if you want to catch more trophy fish and have more fun while you're doing it, you will benefit from this *Fishing Central California* guidebook. Whether you're new to fishing, or an accomplished angler, this comprehensive and entertaining guide will improve your chances every time you wet a line in California and beyond.

With first-hand breakdowns of the region's top fisheries, and some interesting stories about these unique waters along the way, this foolproof manual reveals the secrets to catching your favorite species—from bass and trout, to salmon and sharks. Unlike many fishing guides, this informative book is written by a local author, longtime Central California angler Brian Milne, who knows the ins and outs of the area's small streams, rivers, lakes and ocean fisheries. That's why you won't find any ratings or opinionated takes on the waters presented in this book because each of the fine fisheries the author has selected

are productive ones when the right methods are used. And this book will help you find the correct approach with an objective look at the best ways to catch bigger and better fish on the waters you love.

You will also learn how to:

- Read water and how weather and seasons affect a bite.
- Select the right baits, lures and equipment for particular fish and situations.
- Recognize underwater behaviors and adjust your techniques accordingly.
- Master proper lure and bait presentations for the unique fisheries.
- Turn a tough day into a great one with tons of tips and tricks.

Packed with knowledge, interesting features, rules and regulations, and amusing and instructive fishing tales, *Fishing Central California* is the best fishing guide you'll find for this area.

A leopard shark landed by the author at Morro Bay.

Central California Fisheries

A map of the freshwater waters covered in this guide

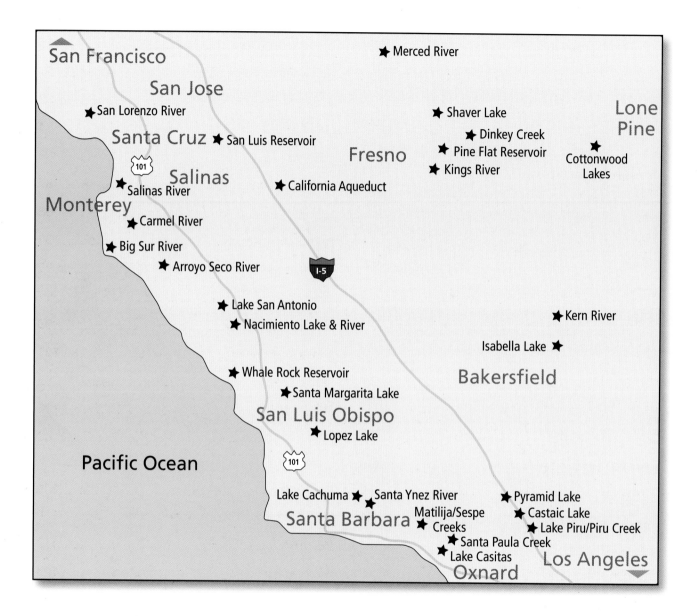

San Francisco

San Jose

Merced River

San Lorenzo River

Shaver Lake

Lone Pine

Santa Cruz ★ San Luis Reservoir

Dinkey Creek

Fresno

Pine Flat Reservoir

Cottonwood Lakes

Salinas

Kings River

Salinas River

California Aqueduct

Monterey

Carmel River

Big Sur River

Arroyo Seco River

I-5

Lake San Antonio

Kern River

Nacimiento Lake & River

Isabella Lake ★

Whale Rock Reservoir

Bakersfield

Santa Margarita Lake

San Luis Obispo

Lopez Lake

Pacific Ocean

101

Lake Cachuma ★ ★ Santa Ynez River

Pyramid Lake

Santa Barbara

Matilija/Sespe Creeks

Castaic Lake

Lake Piru/Piru Creek

Santa Paula Creek

Lake Casitas

Los Angeles

Oxnard

Table of Contents

Acknowledgments

The author and his wife with a trout they both hooked at Nacimiento River.

Fishing Central California is dedicated to my wife, Aja. She's the one who puts up with my fishing addiction, which more often than not takes precedence over yard work, taking out the garbage, and picking up after the dog. Thanks for understanding.

I also want to thank everyone who's fished with me over the years. You are the reason I have so many great fishing stories to share, and I thank you for those. Let's do it again soon.

This book would not be possible if not for the team at No Nonsense Fly Fishing Guidebooks. Thanks for adding this title to your fine list of fishing guides.

Most importantly, I'd like to thank family, my grandparents, sister, Stacy, and parents, Jon and Pat, who taught me how to fish at Lee Vining Creek during an unforgettable trip through Yosemite National Park and Inyo National Forest.

That's where it all started, with a Zebco rod and reel combo and a chunk of cheddar cheese.

I've been hooked ever since.

—Brian Milne

The author as a youth and his father with a trout caught on Lee Vining Creek.

Introduction

For Central California anglers, by a Central California angler

Central California offers some of the most unique fishing opportunities on the West Coast. From the Bay Area down to Ventura County, the fishing possibilities are endless for the saltwater or freshwater angler, fly fisherman or spinning reel angler.

Best of all, the weather usually allows for excellent fishing all year long.

First, there's the Pacific Ocean and the countless miles of precious shoreline access saltwater anglers have. The sport fishing charters have it even better with miles and miles of deep- and shallow-water fisheries filled with trophy-sized game fish such as salmon and albacore, and unbeatable rockcod and lingcod bites along the bottom.

If saltwater fishing isn't your thing, the area's lakes provide stellar bass and trout fishing throughout the four seasons. In Ventura, bass anglers can turn to Lake Casitas. Santa Barbara bassers get their fix at Cachuma, while San Luis Obispo County is spoiled with Lopez and Santa Margarita lakes. North County and Monterey anglers might have it the best with very diverse fisheries in San Antonio and Nacimiento.

Then there are the region's lifelines, its coastal streams and rivers—probably the most overlooked waters in the region. Did you know you can fish Nacimiento River on the old army base at Camp Roberts on certain weekends during the season? Did you know coastal rivers such as the Big Sur are open to fishing for sea-run trout at times

Releasing a native rainbow trout on the North Fork of the Kern River.

during the year? Most anglers in the area don't realize or consider what waters are available. And, we haven't even scratched the surface of what this manual covers.

This fishing guide takes a look at all the top fisheries and the best ways to fish these spectacular spots. Along the way, you'll find additional resources—such as rules and regulations for certain waters and contact information for additional details—as well as tips, techniques and different tactics that are guaranteed to make you a better angler.

Most importantly, this book is written by a conservation-minded angler who takes time to point out some of the best ways to preserve our precious fisheries.

Now, let's get to those fisheries. Please join me on the fishing trip of a lifetime through all the countless locations Central California has to offer.

About the Author

The author fishing as a youngster at Lee Vining Creek.

The author, Brian Milne, has been fishing Central California waters his entire life.

Brian Milne is an avid angler/outdoorsman and writer from San Luis Obispo County, California, where he lives with his wife Aja. Milne has spent nearly his entire life fishing Central California. He is a graduate of local Cuesta College with an associate in arts degree in general studies and Cal Poly San Luis Obispo with a bachelor's degree in journalism.

The California native is an award-winning journalist who has written for a handful of publications in Central California and contributes to fishing magazines such as *California Fishing & Hunting News* and *California Game and Fish.*

A staff writer for *The Tribune* newspaper in San Luis Obispo, Milne is working on additional outdoors guides on the region and can be reached at editor@californiaangler.com. Check out his site, www.CaliforniaAngler.com, for more of his fishing stories.

Useful Tips and Techniques

Preparing for your fishing trip now will help you avoid setbacks once you get to the river's edge.

Spring Training

Using your time wisely during the offseason

Don't let the winter months put a damper on your fishing preparation.

Winter doldrums? I like to call this frigid portion of year spring training.

Winter is the time to tinker with tackle, tie flies, clean reels, repair rods and prepare for the upcoming fishing season.

Whether you're into small-stream trout angling or big-water bassin', nothing makes a wintry evening go by quicker than churning out a few dozen Elk Hair Caddis or cleaning out that ol' tackle box of yours.

Preparing your fishing gear for the spring now will surely save you some headaches in the future. Migraines like opening your tackle box streamside for the first time only to find your salmon eggs have turned into red BBs, your petrified PowerBait might as well be "PaperWeight," and your plastic worms have melted into a glittery gob of goo.

Here's a checklist that can help you get through the so-called winter doldrums and get you primed for a productive spring.

Repair the Rods

Take a good look at your fishing rods, which will be the backbone of your fishing experience this spring.

Start at the tip, which sees most of the abuse throughout the year and slowly check the remainder of the rod for anything out of the ordinary such as a chip, a dent, or even a (gulp) crack.

After going over the rod itself, check the guides for hairline cracks or inconsistencies that can damage fishing line. One way to find cracks in guides is to run a cotton swab or Q-tip inside the guides. If the swab or tip sticks, a crack could be in the works.

You can repair rods yourself with any of the numerous repair kits on the market or take it to a shop to get the work done by experts. Do it now in the offseason, or you could go weeks without it during the season.

For do-it-yourself anglers, Rodsmith makes repair kits for everything from damaged guides and tiptops to replacement handle kits, reel seats, grips, butt caps and winding checks. Bass Pro Shops, Cabela's, Fuji, Pac Bay, and others also offer various rod tip and handle repair kits.

Ready the Reels

If the rod is the backbone, the reel is the heart of your fishing outfit. Give your reels the respect they deserve this winter. In fact, go over your reels two or three times if need be.

First, it's important to clean out any sand or dirt with an old rag or cloth. This will keep your reels free spinning and ensure accurate casting year-round. Just be sure to use plenty of care when taking reels apart and take note of which parts go where.

After wiping down the interior parts, be sure to add a drop of oil to the ball bearings to keep the unit running smoothly (Abu Garcia Reel Oil is a good choice). Avoid applying excess oil as it can drip onto the spool and affect casting.

You might want to strip your line off altogether when working on a reel.

Abu Garcia also makes a Silicote Reel Lube that helps protect reels against wear and corrosion in-season. Quantum Hot Sauce lube is another favorite among bass anglers.

Last, but not least, change out your line to prevent future heartbreak. Don't risk losing trophy fish by using old, worn-out, or weathered line.

Many tournament anglers replace their lines prior to every event.

Spring Trip Checklist

Now that you're making that much-anticipated trip to the Sierra, here are some last-minute tips that will make the trip a success:

Waterproof waders and float tubes: Make sure they don't have leaks, or it's going to be a long trip. You'll also want to pack extra fleece underwear becasuse you'll be wading in snowmelt.

Replace your line: Replace that old line so "the fish of the day" doesn't become "the one that got away." Six-pound line from last year is probably about as strong as 2-pound test this year. Fly fishermen should check their fly line for cracks and replace leaders and spools of tippet.

Check your reels: Make sure they're clean and lubricated so the reel spins freely.

Examine your rod: Most importantly, check to make sure your rod isn't cracked, bent and that the guides are in tip-top condition. Always consider bringing a backup rod and leaving it in your car in case something happens to your favorite pole.

Sort tackle: Last but not least, sort through your tackle box and only bring what you need for those long hikes. Think small. Smaller lures, hooks and flies always work best in Sierra lakes and rivers. Spincasters can't go wrong with Rooster Tails, Super Dupers, Panther Martins, fresh jars of Salmon Eggs and PowerBait. Fly fisherman always have plenty of Elk Hair Caddis, Hares Ears, Midge nymphs, Pheasant Tails and emergers on hand.

Tying flies in the winter will allow for more time on the water in the spring.

Casual anglers should spool up two to three times a season, while more frequent anglers should consider replacing line on their main and spare reels every couple of fishing trips (especially when fishing for toothy fish or in heavy cover).

When you stow your reel between trips, it's a good idea to loosen the drag to alleviate stress on the line and the drag washers.

Prep the Tackle

The cold months are also an ideal time to maintain your tackle.

Hard plastic lures can be cleaned with soap and water to prevent corrosion or mildew.

Do you have a go-to lure that just doesn't retrieve the way it used to? If the bait still doesn't run true after a cleaning, use a pair of pliers to straighten out the line tie. Misaligned wires on spinnerbaits or buzzbaits might also need straightening.

Old hooks should be checked for rust, or better yet, ditched in favor of stainless steel or red hooks when possible.

Now it's on to the tackle box. If organization hasn't been your thing in recent years, make it a resolution this year.

Instead of just separating the basics—weights from hooks and hard baits from plastics—organize your lures by type (spinnerbaits, buzzbaits and crankbaits) and even color. Knowing where

that go-to lure is without searching will mean fewer missed opportunities when lunkers come swimming by.

If fly fishing is your thing, get started on those new flies. You can never have enough Elk Hair Caddis in that trusty fishing cap of yours. It also wouldn't hurt to clean up those fly boxes and improve on that hodgepodge of a fly-filing system you have in place.

Check the Threads

Yes, even your wardrobe could use a look over—and no, we're not looking for a complete makeover here.

Take your waders to the tub and check for leaks now rather than when you're hopping into that snowmelt in the Sierra Nevada.

Keep an eye out for dry rot, cracks, tears or worn areas around the seams, feet and knees. If waders leak, and they're still under warranty, it's time to send them in for repairs.

If you don't have time, or if the warranty has expired, wader repair kits are inexpensive and easy to use. Sun Set Super Patch cures with sunlight or UV light, while Aqua Seal works without patches or seam tape.

After your waders are ready, take a good look at your wading boots. Check laces for cuts or frays and make sure the soles are ready to make that next trek across the river. If it's time for replacement felt, Simms makes a thick, high-density replacement that's durable and easy to apply on most styles of boots.

Now that your wading outfit is set, wash that dirty old fishing vest of yours and check out clearance racks at your local sporting goods store for new fishing shirts and pants.

Forget style points and stick to earth tones to avoid spooking fish while you're browsing the banks. Plenty of pockets are also a plus when shopping for outdoor attire.

Prepare for Disaster

Once you've given your gear the TLC it deserves, prepare for the worst-case scenario this spring.

On top of a first aid kit, every angler should pack rod and wader repair kits for their fishing trips.

When putting together a rod repair kit, be sure to include such necessities as tape, rubber bands, spare tiptops, guides, split rings, candle/wax stubs along with waterproof matches or a lighter, pliers, safety pins (which can double as a temporary line guide), and heat-set cement or Superglue.

It's also a good idea to have a backup rod and reel on hand along with a few hundred yards of extra line. Better yet, treat yourself to a new rod or reel and use your old setup as a backup this season.

Winter is a great time to consider purchasing a new combo as many retailers discount last year's models for the new year.

With a backup setup in place, and all of your other gear in check, you should be prepared to make this a year to remember on the water.

Making sure your gear is in tip-top shape now will prevent hassles when the spring season starts.

Scouting Report

Studying fisheries at their lowest flows now can net big results later in the year

When the rivers are down, it's time to start scouting out runs for the upcoming season.

Winter's here. Time to pack away the rods and count down the days until spring, right? Wrong.

Now's the time to head out to your favorite river or stream and scout out runs for the upcoming season. A time when you don't even have to string up your rod can be one of your most productive "fishing" days of the year.

Sure, catch rates are typically down along with the early-winter water levels, but if you do your homework in the off-season you're bound to have a field day when late-winter steelhead runs or spring trout openers roll around.

Veteran anglers take advantage of this time of year when rivers are still at their lowest, clearest flows—perfect for taking note of submerged logs, ledges, boulders or other underwater features that are more visible now than they are for much of the year.

In the early winter, most rivers rarely see anglers in this fair-weather state of ours.

Fishermen can use the quiet time to their advantage, working the banks of their favorite stretches in total anonymity, studying the flows and tendencies of its resident fish populations.

The key is to pay attention and take note of all the fine details of the river. Bring along a small notepad to help map out what you see. Or, better yet, take a photo. A good pair of waders and a wading staff will make getting from one side of the river to the other a snap.

Look for anything that strikes you as different, providing habitat for the species you fish. Study everything from endless eddies and side channels of your favorite runs, to the foamy edges of the main currents you rarely consider.

Look for rising fish. If there's a hatch coming off, but you don't notice any takers, you might not be looking closely enough. In the winter, rises are so lazy they barely make a ring. So sit back, and let your eyes do the fishing. Scan for those telltale boils that might only appear today and will surely hint to good fishing below when the water levels soar in coming months.

One good approach when trying to read large or unfamiliar rivers is to break them up into a compilation of smaller, fishable sections rather than one overwhelming mass of water.

First, search the shallow stretches for any places a trout is likely to feel safe. Some ideal holding spots include undercut banks, beneath logs and below overhanging brush or tree branches. These are prime holding spots when rivers swell with snowmelt and leave the water stained and fast-moving, forcing trout to hug the banks in search of protection from the strong currents.

Second, look for areas that will provide fish with food. Find pockets (behind boulders or at the bottom of pools) where trout can camp out and

Pools like this rocky run on the Merced River unveil some telling characteristics in the fall.

Anglers can avoid crowds and take in picturesque scenery when the leaves turn in the fall.

eat without using a ton of energy. Trout are very sluggish this time of year and aren't willing to go out of their way for food. Find a concentration of these winter whoppers holding in a food-carrying current and you've probably stumbled across that "secret spot" for the rest of the year.

Deep pools are obvious big-fish magnets but also see plenty of pressure throughout the year. Look past the bottomless holes and waterfalls and seek out other key strike zones that won't catch your eye later in the year. Note sections where strong currents flow into slower, shallow-water riffles. Or outside bends where current, springs or feeder creeks provide a constant supply of food and refuge from fast-flowing water and direct sunlight.

While the surface is probably the most telling aspect of the river, most of the action comes from below the surface. Take advantage of the low flows to get a feel for the subsurface portion of your favorite stretch of river. Look for runs that bottom out or wind through subtle cavities that could protect hungry holdovers looking for an easy meal. Those perforations are even better when cover is present. Standing waves or eddies can also signal hideouts below where larger fish are seeking refuge.

And don't forget to make a note of the boulders and other structure breaking the surface because they could be submerged once the runoff begins. Large rocks provide pockets downstream and will hold fish all year long. The same goes for large logs, or drops to lower pools.

Once you've gotten those stretches scouted out, be sure to reward yourself with some time on the water, testing your new spots with your favorite fly or lure to catch a little glimpse of what the river's future might hold.

Drop-shot 'Crawlers

Even the most stubborn bass can't help but be enticed by a fat worm

A Santa Margarita Lake largemouth caught on a drop-shot worm near The Narrows.

> *"Good Lord! He'll show up with a coffee can full of worms. Red can, Hills Brothers."*
>
> —Paul Maclean (played by Brad Pitt),
> in *A River Runs Through It*

It's easy to see where Maclean, a lifelong fly-fisherman, was coming from.

I've been lucky enough to fly-fish the big Blackfoot in Missoula, Montana, and there's nothing quite like it. To me, watching a Montana trout rise beats a California sunset any day and an out-of-towner and his can o' worms could put a damper on the whole experience in a hurry.

But this isn't Montana, and we're not talking blue-ribbon trout rivers here. The spring season in the Golden State means one thing: a big bass bonanza is taking place at our lakes. And if you want monster bass, live worms (gulp) might be your best bet, as painful as it is to admit.

I wouldn't be caught dead with night crawlers during a trout-fishing excursion in the Sierra Nevada, but when I can't get away to the mountains there's nothing more exhilarating than landing a lunker largemouth. And it seems there's no better way to entice these stubborn potbellies than to wet a fat, juicy worm.

What ever happened to the good ol' night crawler anyway? Back in the day, the worm was a kid's best friend—a catchall bait for trout, bass, sunfish, catfish and carp.

Nowadays, night crawlers are about as in style as bellbottoms and polyester, but talk to any trophy bass hunter and they'll tell you live bait is usually their number one option.

Why Worms?

Fishing live bait might not be the trendiest approach in this tournament-crazed bass world we live in today, but even legendary bass fishermen Roland Martin admits he's fished with live bait while tracking monster bass.

Martin, who hosts his own television series "Fishing with Roland Martin" and was recently named one of "Top 10 Greatest Anglers" by *Bassmaster*, admitted to a room full of anglers at

Live night crawlers are popular with trophy bass hunters.

the Fred Hall Fishing, Tackle and Boat Show that some of the best bass he's caught came on live bait.

"I've tried everything to catch trophy bass," he said in San Francisco. "I've caught them with night crawlers. I've even tried live crawfish. Some of the biggest bass I've caught came on live bait in situations where anglers had tried everything to fool these fish."

If live bait is good enough for a nine-time BASS Angler of the Year, you'd figure everyone would be chucking worms these days, but that's not the case.

So why doesn't anyone fish worms?

Anglers who believe in the worm, point the finger at the corporate fishing world, which they say is stuck on fishing for big bucks rather than behemoth bass.

According to the American Sportfishing Association, 45 million U.S. anglers spend more than $42 billion a year on fishing tackle, trips and related services with each angler spending an average of $1,046 a year on their craft.

In California, one of the three biggest fishing states (next to Florida and Texas), retail sales of fishing equipment have surpassed $2.4 billion—with only a small percentage of those sales going to night crawlers. The real money is being made on artificial baits. "Go-to lures" like the Castaic T Series swim baits, which can sell for $125, or the Waking Hard Bait by 3:16 Lure Co., which sells for $150.

Night crawlers? Well, worms are lucky to bring in $2.49 at the mom-and-pop bait shops around the corner from your favorite hole, but they can net the same big results as those bulky swimbaits trophy bass anglers live by. Just ask trophy bass hunter Chris Wolfgram, of Suisun, who has caught five double-digit bass and loads of 8- and 9-pounders on night crawlers over the years.

"My biggest is 14.1 pounds," he said, "and it was a fish that everybody had thrown every artificial lure they had to for more than a week with no success. She was completely spawned out, too, some 28 inches long. She should have been over 16 pounds.

"Night crawlers work, I just think they're looked down upon because of corporate brainwashing. Too many people let others make up their mind for them."

Drop-shotting 'Crawlers

I first stumbled across drop-shotting 'crawlers while sight fishing late in the season at Lopez Lake near Arroyo Grande. Thanks to sizzling temperatures in the 100s, the resident bass were stubborn as could be in the crystal-clear Lopez shallows. I tried everything in hopes of provoking a strike—tube baits, crankbaits, swimbaits, minnows, jig-and-pigs, buzzbaits, poppers, spinnerbaits and every style of plastic my pocketbook, and sanity, could afford.

No such luck. When I switched over to night crawlers on a whim, my luck changed drastically. Even the most dogged bass couldn't resist a drop-shot worm and by the end of the week I had caught the biggest bass of my life—what I believe was a 14-pounder that fought like a heavyweight and managed to bust my dinky 10-pound scale.

The only problem with this spawner, which I quickly released despite the fact that it might have surpassed the lake record (13 pounds, 11 ounces by Paul Pierce in March, 2000), was that I caught it by my lonesome. Luckily I brought my tripod along for the ride that day and have proof that drop-shot night crawlers work in tough summer conditions at lakes like Lopez.

"I think 'crawlers will work anywhere worms get washed in the water," Wolfgram said, "which is basically everywhere."

Night crawlers can be fished just about anywhere successfully, although they're fished best near old spawning grounds or mouths of feeder creeks that hold good numbers of fish or a couple of stubborn lunkers that you know of.

While I've had loads of success fishing night crawlers at Central California lakes like Lopez, Santa Margarita, San Antonio, Nacimiento, Casitas, and Cachuma, Wolfgram has done most of his damage fishing gobs of 'crawlers on

The author with a double-digit bass caught at Lopez Lake.

his home lake Berryessa and San Pablo Dam Reservoir in the Bay Area.

"I believe that bass—and nearly every other freshwater fish for that matter—are conditioned to eat 'crawlers right from the start," Wolfgram said. "During every rainy season, millions of 'crawlers are washed into nearly every lake in the country. They're high in protein, have no bones or spines, and take practically no effort to catch—pretty much the perfect snack. Even when a bass has gotten big, and now eats mostly trout fry, or maybe crawfish in the pre-spawn, they often cannot get past that biological imprint on their brains which says, 'all good, easy, safe.'"

Tackle Time

The two basic components of a drop-shot 'crawler rig include a drop weight—round weights snag less often when fished in summer cover—with a quick clip system along with a small, light-wire worm hook tied on with a palomar knot.

Weather conditions, water clarity and depth all determine the amount of weight you should use. In the summer, I like to use a ⅛-ounce weight up to 15 feet. Up to 25 feet, I'll switch to a 5⁄32-ounce sinker and use a 3⁄16 on the rare occasion that I'm fishing deeper than 25 feet.

Depending on where you fish, a medium-action spinning rod with 10- to 15-pound Spiderline Super Mono XXX line is a good bet, although drop-shot specific graphite rods have made the technique easier on the body. Pflueger recently added a pair of 7-foot, ultra-light Trion Series rods (PTCA 4770-2UL and PTSP 4770-2L), which have become popular with anglers whose wrists can get tired easily while using drop-shot and other finesse presentations. But if you know you'll be fishing for lunker bass, a medium- or heavy-action spinning rod will surely get the job done.

One productive drop-shot rig consists of a Bakudan drop weight, which uses a line clip and a round-shaped weight that makes tying your rigs and avoiding hang-ups a snap. The weight also lets you get a good feel for the bottom, and most importantly, strikes from fish.

For a hook, tie on a Gamakatsu G-Lock hook (1/0 to 5/0) a good 36 inches from the weight when fished up to 15 feet. If fishing at depths greater than 15 feet, pinpoint where fish are holding on your finder and adjust your rig

A Lopez Lake lunker caught on a drop-shot worm.

accordingly. The best way to hook the worm is through the head, stringing the length of the hook through the 'crawler.

Another good technique requires a six- to 10-inch strip of black elastic line, which I tie off between the weight and the 3-foot leader to the hook. Adding an elastic strip allows you to put even more action on the worm without having to drag the weight across the bottom, keeping the worm in the strike zone until the angler decides when to tug it out.

Presentation

For starters, flip down your polarized shades and study the shallows for any holding bass. The best time to do this is in the early morning on stretches of the water that are in full sunlight.

If you spot a nice bass, or see a section where bass could be holding, cast beyond the area a good 10 or 15 feet (even if it means casting onto shore) to avoid startling the fish.

Retrieve the rig in a series of short, slow increments no more than a few inches at a time while keeping your rod tip up so you can instantly feel a strike and react.

Once you near the fish, slow down your retrieve considerably and let the weight catch on the bottom, allowing you to work the bait in front of a fish's nose until it provokes a strike. The key for drop-shotting night crawlers is to keep the worm in the strike zone as long as possible, working the bait by manipulating the rod tip with a slight twinge of the wrist.

Getting down the "doodling" method of working a drop-shot rig can take time and plenty of practice. Once you figure it out, you will have mastered an approach that even the most finicky of bass won't be able to resist.

Once that ginormous bass commits, set the hook, check your drag and enjoy the ride.

You never know, a Hills Brothers can o' worms just might make your day.

Rising to the Top

Topwater lures tempt lunkers during the evening hours

Topwater and shallow-running crankbaits can tempt hefty largemouth bass late in the year and late in the day.

Tournament anglers often refer to topwater lures as the "10-percent solution," meaning surface baits can be useless 90 percent of the time.

But during the evening hours of the fall, the tables turn.

The days have gotten shorter and more and more bass fishermen are staying on the lake until dusk, when the topwater bite is just starting to pick up. That's when topwater becomes the "90-percent solution."

"It seems like there are always guys hauling back at closing time this time of year," said Adam Casey, assistant manager the Lake Casitas marina (805) 649-2043. "That's when the fishing is at

its best. The lake usually stays open a half-hour after the sun goes down and the fishing is best right around then. It gets to a point where you want to keep fishing because the topwater bite is so good, but it's so dark you can't stay on the lake any more."

A majority of the time, evening bass anglers at Casitas and other Central California lakes are throwing topwater lures and shallow-running crankbaits. And they're throwing hard baits for two reasons: They're as productive as they are fun to throw.

"Topwater is absolutely the most fun way to catch fish," Casey added. "It's fun because you're always on the move. That's the thing people don't like about fishing, just sitting there and waiting all the time. With topwater lures and crankbaits, you're always on the move."

Noisy hardbaits make lunker largemouth pounce in the fall. And more often than not, it doesn't matter what you throw once the sun starts to go down. If it hits the surface right, topwater lures and shallow-water crankbaits are going to provoke reaction strikes for boat anglers and shore fishermen alike.

In the fall, bass make their seasonal move into shallow breaks, coves and tributary creeks in search of baitfish. So the best baits resemble shad, are fast moving and make plenty of noise. Lipless crankbaits seem to have the best shape, color and wiggle for fishing the lower-level lakes in early to mid autumn. A silver Rat-L-Trap, Strike King Diamond Shad Premier, Cotton Cordell Super Spot or the various patterns made by Lucky Craft are good shad look-alikes. Small-lipped crankbaits like the various Rapalas, the Stanford Cedar Shad, Abu Garcia Tormentors and Reaction Innovations Method Cranks also produce solid results.

A largemouth caught on a Fat Rap just after sundown.

The key for all of the above baits is to draw the attention of the bass. Bright colors, like chartreuse or hot orange, are great attention-getters and help baits stand out in a dimly lit environment. Large baits are also a good because chunkier baits are easier for bass to spot and strike. The bigger baits also mean bigger fish, although don't be surprised if you pull up an occasional juvenile at the end of the day.

"You'll catch all kinds of sizes with big baits," Casey said, "even the smaller, dumber fish because they don't know any better."

As far as topwater lures are concerned, there are three types that come in handy in the fall: walkers, poppers and weedless baits.

Walkers look like narrow, lipless crankbaits and slide across the surface with walk-the-dog action and rely on the built-in movement to draw strikes. Good walkers include the Rapala Skitter or Berkley Frenzy Walker.

Poppers plop their way across the surface thanks to a concave face that splashes water off the surface like a spooked school of shad. The Original Pop-R is the best popper on the market, although Rapala (Skitter Pop), Berkley (Frenzy Popper) and Lucky Craft (Bevy Popper) have their own variations.

Weedless baits, like the Sumo Frog or Marsh Mouse, are best used around weeds, algae and the pads.

Casey is a big fan of all the topwater options because they offer a solution for almost every situation, which makes you wonder why they've been deemed a "10-percent solution."

"With a topwater, all you have to do is match the spot you're fishing," he said. "You cast to that spot, see a bass exploding at the surface and your line takes off. Man, that's the way to go."

Saltwater:
Near and Deep Sea
Coastal Fisheries

The author with a 5-foot leopard shark caught off a kayak out of Morro Bay.

Rockcod Fishing

It's tough to beat the deep sea fishing off the Central Coast

Rockfish can be caught off the shore or via charter boats from Santa Barbara to Monterey.

The Central Coast rockcod bite is often so wide open when unlocked by the Department of Fish and Game that anglers don't want to think about anything else.

Not even salmon, albacore, halibut or sharks draw the same amount of enthusiasm as the lingcod, red rockcod, cabezon and assorted rockfish that define this region.

The main focus of Patriot Sportfishing (805) 595-7200 out of Avila Beach, and Virg's Landing (805) 772-1222 in Morro Bay, is usually the nearshore fisheries off the coast from Santa Barbara to San Simeon.

Rockcod trips range from $30–200 depending on time spent on the water and are usually the most productive off the coast of San Simeon.

"There's very little fishing pressure up there," said Mike Forrest of Virg's Landing, "so that's where some dandy fish are caught."

Virg's 4- to 8-hour trips usually revolve around the local reefs located about 10 miles off the coast of Morro Bay. The 10- to 12-hour and overnight trips reach as far north as Cape San Martin and Point Sur. Along with anchovies and squid, saltwater anglers also turn to plastics, spoons and live bait for the larger fish.

The most popular setup includes one or more shrimp fly rigs (depending on current regulations) tipped with anchovy or squid chunks. A 2-ounce fire tiger Gibbs Minnow with a single or treble hook can double as a weight and often attracts larger species such as lingcod or cabezon.

"It's wide open for rockcod year-round," Forrest added. When the season is open, "we can get some big fish even on our shorter trips."

But more often than not, the rockcod fishing is not open the entire year and is regularly closed by the Department of Fish and Game. When the rockcod fishery is closed, boat-based anglers in the Morro Bay South-Central management area are not permitted to fish for federal groundfish and associated state-managed species, including rockfish, lingcod, cabezon, sheephead, ocean whitefish, scorpionfish, and other species.

Divers and shore-based fishermen, however, are sometimes permitted to catch groundfish through certain portions of the closure. The Department of Fish and Game's definition of shore-based anglers is those who "fish from beaches, banks, piers, jetties, breakwaters, docks and other manmade structures connected to the shore."

For the most current information on state recreational groundfishing regulations, go to www.dfg.ca.gov/mrd/fishing_map.html or call the regulations hotline at (831) 649-2801.

Rockcod are a top target of anglers fishing outside of Morro Bay with Virg's Landing.

Santa Cruz Island is a popular destination because it is located only 20 miles from Ventura Harbor.

Ventura Saltwater

Limits are the norm when rockcod fishing is allowed off the Ventura coast to depths of 360 feet.

Deeper water typically means bigger fish for salty anglers trying to get in as many hours on the water as possible before the water and fishing cools off in the winter.

All year long, anglers can expect to catch quality red snapper, lingcod and sculpin along with the rockcod, calico bass and sand bass, says Jim Clark, general manager at Channel Islands Sportfishing Center (805) 382-1612.

Clark added that a few exotic species can be picked up when the temperatures drop down into the mid-60s near the Channel Islands.

When hunting for new saltwater species, try tossing large, weighted plastic baits—even freshwater lures created for lunker largemouth or striped bass will work as search baits in shallower regions around the islands and Santa Barbara coast. More and more lure makers are creating plastic baits for saltwater anglers, including Offshore Angler, which has a growing arsenal of plastics that includes shrimp, squid and shad look-alikes.

Octopus hooks with live anchovies, sardines or mackerel will work for nearly all species if fished at the correct depth or near balls of baitfish.

Saltwater anglers should take note of ever-changing groundfish regulations.

Monterey Bay Saltwater

The Monterey County coast is a unique fishery in that it has nearly the same impressive rockcod fishing as the San Simeon and Morro Bay coast, but anglers can also catch some great albacore, bonito and Chinook salmon runs during different times of the year.

And if that isn't enough, Monterey anglers can also search for crabs late in the year.

The crab season typically opens in early November with popular sportfishing outfits like Chris' Landing (831) 375-5951 offering regular rockcod-crab combo trips in the winter months.

"We get some nice Dungeness crabs, usually about three to a person," said Todd Archoleo of Chris' Landing. "There's some good rockcod and big lingcod up here too."

Limits are common for rockcod fishing with an occasional lingcod pushing 20 pounds when the conditions are calm.

Other common species in the Monterey Bay area include sanddab, halibut, lingcod, kelp greenling, white croaker and perch.

When fishing for these larger species be sure to use rigs that are tied with 20-pound test line or heavier. Most rockcod rigs are tied with nothing less than 30-pound test and will work for other species as well.

For up-to-date information on groundfishing regulations, call the regulations hotline at (831) 649-2801.

A shallow-water rockfish caught around a kelp bed just north of San Simeon.

Shark Fishing

When rockcod fishing slows, party boats and even kayakers switch to sharks

A nice leopard shark caught on anchovies out of Morro Bay.

When the rockcod fishery is closed by the Department of Fish and Game, Virg's Landing in Morro Bay is always searching for new ways to help anglers feed their saltwater appetite.

When the season closes, Virg's often offers shark and sanddab trips a couple of times a week, with soupfin, leopard and dog sharks making up most of the shark catches. Anglers can also fish for mackerel and sanddabs along the way.

Kayak anglers, who are not always exempt from rockcod closures, also switch gears and fish for sharks or halibut in and around Morro Bay. Kayakers usually hook up with leopard and smoothhound sharks in the 3- to 5-foot range.

Anglers in search of sharks dead drift anchovies near schools of baitfish. They may also fish the sandy flats for sanddabs, butter sole, curlfin sole, flathead sole, rex sole, rock sole, sand sole and starry flounder with smaller than #2 hooks and no more than two-pound weights.

Other Saltwater Species

Salmon, halibut, and albacore fishing in the Central Coast region

Saltwater anglers can also fish for salmon, halibut and albacore off the Central Coast.

Central Coast saltwater anglers don't usually know what to expect when salmon season opens in April.

Because of frequent rockcod closures, few fishing boats leave the docks early in the year. The little information anglers have to work with usually comes from nearshore sanddab trips and whale watching excursions.

"We really don't have any indication on whether we have (salmon) or not," said Jim Nielsen of Patriot Sportfishing (805) 595-7200 in Avila Beach. "It's one of those deals where you have to go out and look around for 'em a few days before the season opens.

"Salmon are such a day-to-day deal. It's not good to go out and look for them early because they could be gone tomorrow."

Scout boats should be on the lookout for birds feeding in waters that are full of bait. That's where you'll find sprinklings of salmon feeding in areas off the San Luis Obispo and Monterey coast. The Central Coast/Southern California region spans from Pigeon Point (near Santa Cruz) to the Mexico border.

Anglers are usually allowed a two-fish limit. The retention of coho, or silver salmon, is prohibited and all salmon that are less than 24 inches must be released immediately because of state regulations. Salmon fishermen are also limited to one rod and line and two single-point, single-shank barbless hooks when fishing north of Point Conception.

In recent years, proven spoons like the Krocodile and hoochies, or bait, have produced during the chinook dawn bite off the Santa Barbara and San Luis Obispo coast.

In Monterey, most of the boats mooch, instead of troll, in about 150 feet of water.

Farther south, fish can be found much closer to the surface and seem to prefer deeper water—which calls for larger spoons and slower action—during sunny, mid-day time periods.

Work the birds, which can be a dead giveaway that baitfish, and potential salmon, are present. If surface-oriented birds are present, fish the first 20-30 feet. If birds are diving, try deeper baits.

Yellowtail are usually found in the warmer waters off the coast of Baja and San Diego but a few have been picked up off the Central Coast in recent years.

"The main two factors are water clarity and bait," Nielsen said. "We look for dirtier water with a lot of bait. That's where you'll have the most luck."

A coho identification page can be found at www.dfg.ca.gov/mrd/oceansalmon.html.

Tuna Time

Albacore don't typically migrate to the Central Coast until mid to late June.

"It depends on water currents," said Brian Gardner of Patriot Sportfishing. "They're usually looking for warmer water."

During a good run, boats will travel as far as five hours and 100 miles to find a school.

When the water is really warm, Central Coast anglers might even run into a rare yellowtail.

In August 2005, a pair of local anglers said they picked up two rare yellows trolling near kelp paddies "in the albacore zone." One was in the 25-pound class while the second was around 10 pounds.

Because of the cold waters off Central and Northern California, there have been only a handful of yellowtail catches reported off the coast of San Luis Obispo County in the last decade.

Yellowtail are more common in Southern California and Baja California. The fish, which are known for their great fighting ability, are also picky eaters, which can explain the low catch rates in the area. Sometimes yellows will only hit live mackerel. Other times they'll hit exclusively on metal jigs or spoons, fished as fast as an angler can possibly reel.

While there is an outside shot at catching a prized yellowtail, albacore are more common when the tuna make their annual swing through the Central Coast.

During a good run, catch rates have typically been around an albacore or two (in the 10- to 30-pound class) to an angler. Those numbers can increase for private boaters with fewer anglers on board.

For the most part, you can catch a Virg's Landing tuna trip departing out of Morro Bay on Fridays at 11 p.m. for a fare of $200. Contact Virg's (805) 772-1222 for more information or to set up a reservation.

Halibut Fishing

The halibut bite typically picks up in late May, especially out of Port San Luis where Port Side Marine has its Annual Halibut Derby in the summer months.

In years past, as many as 85 anglers have turned out for the tournament with division winners receiving merchandise and cash prizes. One year, the winner, Joe Vaughan, took home a total purse of $2,384.26 for the weekend. A percentage of the tournament profits go to the Central Coast Salmon Enhancement project and various charities.

Contact Port Side Marine at (805) 595-7214 for more information on halibut fishing or annual flattie tournament. Virg's Landing and Patriot Sportfishing also launch halibut trips when salmon and rockcod fishing dies down, especially during the rockcod closures and when halibut begin to enter the bays to spawn.

As far as private boaters are concerned, it's not uncommon for private parties to collectively haul in a hundred or so halibut in a week with some flatties reaching 30-plus pounds.

Central Coast saltwater anglers can pick up an assortment of flatfishes off the coast, including halibut, guitarfish, batrays, sanddabs, and skates.

The most popular setup for halibut is a pre-tied, 20-pound test Pacific Catch halibut rig, which allows the fish to pick up the bait and move off with it without feeling the weight of the sinker.

Halibut are a particular species that prefers live bait, instead of frozen fish and squid, and rarely makes an immediate strike. When you feel a fish begin to take the bait, count to five before attempting to set the hook. Better yet, keep the reel in free spool and let the fish hook itself during the initial run. Be patient and expect to lose a couple of fish before you get hooked up. Once you do, you'll forget all about previous misses as halibut often fight with the best of them.

Be sure to keep pliers within reach as halibut can get a bit nasty once they're in the boat.

Pier Fishing

Who needs a boat when you have the pier?

A pair of winter saltwater anglers fishing off the pier in Santa Barbara.

It's not as glamorous as fly fishing for rainbow trout in the Sierras.

It doesn't have the same appeal as tackling trophy tuna in the deep sea.

But pier fishing along the California coast is less expensive, easier to master and can be equally rewarding.

Especially when you consider:

- Pier anglers regularly catch some of the same sought-after species that charters seek, including halibut, rockfish and even sharks.
- Pier fishing is free in most instances along the Central Coast.

- No fishing license is required in most cases because most piers are public property.
- Most Central California piers are also open 24 hours a day, which gives anglers a legal means of wetting their line after work and provides an opportunity to hook up with the large nocturnal feeders that patrol the shallows.
- Plus it's a lot harder to get seasick on a pier than it is on an afternoon charter boat.

The following are some of the region's most popular pier fishing destinations:

Port Hueneme Pier

Directions: Take Highway 1 and exit Hueneme Road west until you hit the port. Turn left on Ventura Road, another left on Surfside Drive and continue straight until you reach the pier.

Notes: Bait fishing around Pt. Hueneme can be a challenge but bring along some frozen anchovies or squid and the fishing should hold up. Another good technique for catching bait is to bring as many different bait rigs as possible, including traditional Sabikis, feathered hooks, perch baits tied with red and yellow yarn and the various shrimp and squid imitations on the market. The pier is open 24 hours and is better protected than some along the coast and still offers an outside shot at a small sand or leopard shark. Crabbing can also be fun out of Port Hueneme.

Santa Barbara/Sterns Wharf Pier

Directions: Take the 101 to Santa Barbara, exit at State Street and head west, following the signs to the pier/beach.

Notes: Similar fishing to nearby Port Hueneme and Goleta piers, with off-and-on calico and sand bass bites. Sterns can provide a better escape from the afternoon winds that may pick up. Both the Goleta and Santa Barbara piers are equipped with lights for night fishing. Try fishing with large chunks of fresh-cut jacks or anchovies for a shot at a batray, guitarfish, skate, or if you're lucky, a halibut or shark.

Goleta Point Pier

Directions: Take the 101 north of Santa Barbara to Goleta and take the UC Santa Barbara exit to Sandspit Road.

Notes: A fine spot for calico and sand bass, along with your typical surfperch, halibut and sanddabs. If you're not into flatfish, try rigging up some large chunks of frozen squid (you can purchase some at local grocery stores) for bigger rays, sharks

Small surfperch and jacksmelt are common catches off Pismo Pier in Pismo Beach.

and skates. Goleta sees less pressure than the pier at the wharf, especially in the evenings and when UCSB is not in session.

Pismo Beach Pier

Directions: Take the 101 to Pismo Beach and take the Five Cities Drive/Price Street exit to the middle of town. Head west down Pomeroy to the pier parking lot.

Notes: The top catch at Pismo, along with most San Luis Obispo County piers, is barred surfperch and jacksmelt caught on a Sabiki or shrimp flies. Fish the pier supports and breaks for multiple types of surfperch. While trophy catches are rare, the photo wall near the bait shop shows an occasional bat ray, shovelnose guitarfish and even a leopard shark aren't out of the question. Pismo Beach is known as the "Clam Capital of the World," but don't use any Pismo clams for bait because it is illegal in most cases to harvest clams at this clam preserve. This pier is usually open 24 hours.

Avila and Hartford Piers

Directions: Take the 101 north of Pismo Beach and take the Avila Beach Drive exit. Head west on Avila Beach Drive until you reach the pier parking lot on the left.

Notes: The protected cove and an abundance of baitfish makes Avila a great late-night getaway for halibut, bat rays, leopard and swell sharks (also called puffers), smoothhounds, guitarfish and skates. For flatties, fish the bottom using a halibut leader rigged with a whole anchovy (hooked through the nose of the fish) or a freshly caught perch or smelt. Medium hooks tipped with slices of frozen squid can catch everything from sharks to good-sized croaker on calm evenings. The piers at Port San Luis are open 24 hours.

Puffer sharks can be caught off protected bay piers.

Morro Bay T-Piers

Directions: Take Highway 1 north of San Luis Obispo and exit at Morro Bay Boulevard. Go west to Main Street. Turn right and continue to Beach Street, turn left to the embarcadero.

Notes: The north and south T-piers aren't as popular as the piers to the north and south but a chance to catch a rare red snapper, bocaccio, jacksmelt, perch and random rockfish can make it a worthwhile trip. These piers do, however, see lots of pressure because they're located just outside Virg's Landing in Morro Bay.

Cayucos Pier

Directions: Take Highway 1 to the Cayucos Drive exit, which leads straight to the pier parking lot.

Notes: Like the San Simeon Pier, jacksmelt are the hot bite when schools are coming through, although there is said to be a nice halibut bite around the pier when the conditions are calm. If you're lucky, a fat flattie might just take you for a ride. Don't expect to land one unless you have a crab net on hand. The pier is open 24 hours a day and, like the Pismo and San Simeon piers, attracts tourists throughout the year, mainly because Hearst Castle is located a few miles up Highway 1.

San Simeon Pier

Directions: Take Highway 1 north of Cayucos and exit left at San Simeon State Beach.

Notes: Sam Simeon is a great getaway along one of the most beautiful stretches of highway the state has to offer. Hearst Castle gets most of the attention around these parts but don't count out the surfperch and jacksmelt fishing. If your reel is packed with plenty of line, you can reach the larger fish that cruise the kelp beds sprinkled along the coastline. The pier is open 24 hours a day.

The San Simeon Pier provides good fishing for jacks and various surfperch.

Monterey Wharf Piers

Directions: Take Highway 1 to the central Monterey exit and follow Del Monte Avenue to Figueroa Street and stay left until you hit the wharf.

Notes: When the smelt and mackerel are schooling, the fishing can be great. If not, the all-around fishing suffers and makes finding live baitfish difficult. When fishing piers that see lots of pressure like Monterey it's best to bring a wide variety of baits. Anything that sets your rig apart from the pack is a good choice, especially if it resembles some of the fishery's resident baitfish, crabs or shrimp.

Pier Tackle and Techniques

Pier anglers turn to an assortment of techniques and tackle depending on conditions and the species they're hunting.

Anglers in search of a quick nibble typically rig up their favorite surf fishing rig—a popular choice is the Sabiki Rig—on a light-medium action rod. With Sabikis, anglers typically fish straight down or a few feet from the railing, jigging the rig up and down in hopes of hooking perch, smelt and small rockfish around the breaks.

Anglers searching for larger species go with larger saltwater rods and reels with 150 to 200 yards of 15- to 25-pound test line. Baits vary from anchovies, squid, mussels, clams and crabs, and sometimes include artificial soft baits, spoons or feather-fly rockfish rigs.

Pier fishing veterans will bring a pail or bucket along with an aerator for holding fish/bait, along with a crab net, which helps haul in larger fish that would regularly snap your line halfway up the pier.

And bring a camera. The best part about pier fishing in the fall is the fact that you never know what to expect. One minute you're catching a couple of jacks for bait. The next thing you know you're getting spooled by a whopper halibut or shark. And that'll beat a summer trout excursion any time.

Surf Fishing

You can fish for perch at just about every public beach along the coast

A fisherman searching for barred surfperch just north of the San Simeon Pier.

When saltwater fishing slows in the winter because of state-mandated rockcod closures or rough weather conditions, saltwater anglers often turn to the beach for spawning surf fish.

While surf fishing can be good all year long, the wide range of winter tides are perfect for large spawning fish, especially scrappy barred surfperch that can push 12 inches and 2 pounds in some areas along the Central Coast.

While most anglers from San Diego to Santa Cruz resort to pier fishing for the large perch with vertical bronze bars and spots on each side, wader-clad surf fishermen can have the most luck from the shoreline. That's where the big ones can be found, swimming in schools along the breaks.

Silver, calico, redtail and smaller walleye surfperch can also be caught up and down the coast, with your best bet for catching barred perch coming from Pismo Beach to San Simeon.

In Morro Bay, anglers haul in barred perch on mud shrimp, sand crabs and plastic grubs.

Surfperch Fishing

What: Central Coast Barred Surfperch

Where: Santa Barbara to Santa Cruz.

Why: Tasty, spirited fish reach 12 inches and 2 pounds

Tackle: 8- to 11-foot rod, 10- to 15-pound test, leader with red size 4 hooks

Bait: Shrimp, sand crabs and Power Grubs (motor oil, red fleck)

Barred surfperch caught in Morro Bay on a shrimp-style grub.

Rubber lipped and rainbow perch can be caught farther north in the Monterey Bay area with pile worms near rock piles and kelp beds.

If the wind picks up, or the weather turns sour, perch often hug the shoreline of inner bays where the water is calm.

A good catchall bait in most conditions seems to be motor oil grubs with gold or red flakes. Scented attractants such as shrimp- or crawfish-smelling baits can also help pick up the action.

Fly fishermen catch fish on streamers and various crab and shrimp flies and always have a chance to hook up with stripers, halibut or other nearshore species.

The larger barred surfperch typically come from the waters above Morro Bay in Cayucos and Cambria and it isn't uncommon to see a dozen or so fishermen working the same stretch of beach when the tides are retreating, the waves are calm and the weather is ideal.

Most anglers use spinning reels and 8- to 11-foot rods, strung up with 10- to 15-pound test line with a surf leader that includes size 4 or 6 hooks and a pyramid weight. But the size and weight of tackle should correlate with conditions such as the drift, tide and wave height, and frequency.

Surfperch often swim in schools along piers and in the surf zone.

Freshwater:
Lakes, Reservoirs,
Rivers, and Streams

Lopez Lake is known for kicking out solid bass like this double-digit lunker landed by the author.

Arroyo Seco River

A small, challenging fishery located in Monterey County

This is about as tricky a river as you'll find on the Central Coast. Located in a steep, brushy gorge, it is nearly impossible to fish early in the regular trout season because the river swells with runoff.

This Monterey County fishery is located near Salinas and not too far from the heavily populated Silicon Valley. The river runs by a popular campground and receives lots of fishing pressure, even though this section of the river is off limits during the general trout season.

There are two designated sections of water, an upper and a lower section.

The upper water is the stretch above the main waterfall and footbridge, 3.5 miles upstream from the bridge at the U.S. Forest Service Ranger Station. This area is open from the last Saturday in April through November 15. Anglers must hike 3.5 miles up from the campground to fish legally at this time of year.

Fishing on the Arroyo Seco can be tough because of the brushy banks.

Getting to Arroyo Seco

The lower section can be accessed via the 101 and Arroyo Seco Road (County Road G16) from the small town of Greenfield. The upper Arroyo Seco River is accessible from Milpitas Road and Indians Road through Fort Hunter-Liggett.

The trail to the upper reaches is an old fire road located at the end of the campground. It parallels the river for a couple of miles before a narrow single track drops down to the water's edge. Some of the hike requires some wading, so bring waders and a wading staff.

Anglers who make the trek above the waterfall usually lead off with standard dry flies on a floating line as these fish see little pressure and few bugs. If these fish aren't rising, switch to tiny attractor patterns or work the deeper pools with a bead-head nymph. The fishing usually improves farther upstream.

The lower water includes the water below the waterfall located 3.5 miles upstream from the U.S. Forest Service Ranger Station. This lower section is not open during the general trout season. Nearby lakes are open. The lower stretches of the river may be open during the general coastal steelhead season from December to early March on Wednesdays and weekends. Only barbless hooks may be used and fish must be released unharmed. A steelhead report card is also required.

Like many coastal steelhead waters, the Department of Fish and Game often closes particular stretches because of low-flow restrictions. Call (831) 649-2886 for the latest flow information and check current steelhead updates.

The key to fishing Arroyo Seco is to use a stealthy approach and precise casting to avoid hang-ups in overhanging brush and trees.

Big Sur, Carmel, and San Lorenzo Rivers

Steelhead fishing on the "Big Three"

Coastal trout like this juvenile migrate to the sea and return to spawn as steelhead.

The holiday season marks the time of year anglers start seeking out early-winter steelhead along the central coast.

And after some down years in the region, steelhead fishermen hope the heavy rains of the 2004–05 seasons help bolster future steelhead runs.

In the central region, the San Lorenzo River is usually the best indicator of what to expect from the season. The steelhead numbers should continue to improve thanks to "fish recycling," as the past few years have been catch and release only for the silver bullets of these waters. And unlike their king salmon cousins, a fraction of these southern steelhead return to the ocean after spawning. That's why it is important that anglers use extreme care when catching and releasing these precious fish.

Be sure to use barbless hooks and abide by Department of Fish and Game regulations. Fishing is typically open on weekends, Wednesdays and legal holidays from December through early March.

In addition to a fishing license, steelhead anglers must have a valid steelhead report card, available at fishing and sporting goods stores. Be sure to check current regulations (www.dfg.ca.gov) as regulations can change from year to year on these precious steelhead waters.

The Carmel River's low flow restriction is normally around 80 cubic feet per second and applies to the adjacent San Jose, Gibson, Malpaso, and Soberanes creeks.

The Big Sur River, Limekiln Creek and its tributaries, and those portions of Big Sur Coast

The Big Sur River often gets lost in the surrounding coastal beauty.

streams west of Highway 1 from Granite Creek south to Salmon Creek can be closed if Big Sur River flows are less than 40 CFS or if steelhead numbers decline.

Three other Bay Area creeks—Pinole Creek in Contra Costa County, Codornices Creek in Alameda County and Upper Penitencia Creek in Santa Clara County—have been closed to fishing in recent years in order to protect dwindling steelhead runs.

Call the DFG low flow closure hotline (831) 649-2886 for current flows and closures. The message is supposed to be updated Tuesdays and Fridays throughout the season.

The DGF has installed angler survey boxes along several coastal streams to assist in steelhead research. Anglers are asked to fill out the surveys after every trip.

"We're looking for information such as the number of hours fished, number and size of fish caught, and type of equipment used," said DFG Associate Fishery Biologist Mike Hill. "This will help us determine if fishing pressure is having any impact on steelhead populations and allow us to adjust the regulations if necessary."

A closer look at "The Big Three" of Monterey and Santa Cruz counties:

Big Sur River

The Big Sur River is located along one of the most beautiful stretches of coastline in North America—Highway 1 along Monterey's scenic Big Sur Coast.

And, if you hit the Big Sur during the right time, it can be one of the most rewarding experiences an angler will encounter.

"It gets a significant number of fish, but they move through the system very quickly because the spawning area is so limited," according to Geoff Malloway of Central Coast Flyfishing. "Timing is everything. The run, however, is very consistent from one year to the next."

Big Sur trout typically look for riffles in 4 to 6 feet of water. From the shore, with 10- to 12-pound test line, try spinning Blue Fox and Panther Martin lures, or bounce roe baits with krill, Woolly Buggers or Silver Hiltons.

When the water level is down, think small. When water levels jump and water clarity becomes an issue, turn to bigger and brighter presentations. Three primary colors to consider are pink, orange and chartreuse.

The Big Sur, closed to fishing within Pfeiffer Big Sur State Park, is sometimes opened to fishing from late May through October above the upstream end of the gorge pool at the boundary of the park and the Ventana Wilderness Area. Anglers are encouraged to double check the rules and boundaries with the ranger staff to keep in line with the current regulations.

Small wild trout make up a majority of the catches on these coastal steelhead waters.

San Lorenzo River

The San Lorenzo River in Santa Cruz probably gets the biggest, earliest runs of "The Big Three" and also sees the most pressure because it is located closest to the Silicon Valley.

The fishable stretch runs from the mouth to the Lomond Street Bridge in Boulder Creek. Highway 9, off of Highway 1, offers the best access and parallels much of the river.

Malloway, of Central Coast Fly Fishing, suggests fly fishermen fling an olive, bead-headed Woolly Bugger with a floating line. Stripping a Spin-N-Glo is another option.

Using roe and a puffball can also be a good combination, although Malloway encourages anglers to avoid bait altogether.

"Bait, of course, is effective where legal to use," Malloway notes, "but since all fish must be released, I would avoid using bait due to the higher potential of hooking mortality."

Carmel River

The Carmel continues to bounce back from a decade-long closure and was reopened to winter steelhead anglers in 1997.

"The run is more stable than it has been due to a lot of hard work by a few conservation-minded sportsmen, the Monterey Peninsula Water Management District and the DFG, but a lot more work needs to be done," Malloway said of his home water.

The Carmel may be the best fly fishing stretch of "The Big Three," which is good news given the river is an artificial-only water.

Spinners and spoons are also good bets. Try Wiggle Warts, Hot Shots, Kastmasters, Glo Bugs and Kwikfish if you're not into fly fishing.

Access is best at Garland Park, Carmel River State Beach and most of the bridges that cross the river up to Rosie's Bridge.

"This river has some very good fly fishing water that permits traditional casting," Malloway concludes. "Keep in mind that a lot of the fishable water is brushy, so drifting with a floating line is difficult if not impossible. Sink-tip lines are popular, but a floating line with a long leader and a bead-head nymph or an egg pattern can be deadly in the hands of experienced fly fishers."

Lake Cachuma

Trout and largemouth are top draws at this Santa Barbara-area lake

Lake Cachuma can be a fine fishery before the afternoon winds come on.

Anglers come to Lake Cachuma for two reasons—trout and bass. It's as simple as that. The trout bite usually improves along with the water clarity at this Santa Barbara-area lake.

January and February can be slow, murky months for trout anglers, but those days change with better weather, less runoff and additional trout plants by the Department of Fish and Game.

Bass can be had year-round, but many anglers turn to trolling for trout when water temperatures drop in the winter. Most of the trout they catch are half-pounders. Holdovers, however, will track larger lures and may push 3 pounds.

"The trout bite's usually pretty good," said Scott Mangler of the boat dock staff (805) 688-4040. "Everyone catches fish between 16 and 18 inches."

Getting to Cachuma

From Santa Barbara, take the 101 to San Marcos Pass/Highway 154. The park entrance is about 20 miles away on the right.

Most boaters target rainbows down to about 20 feet. Popular trolling patterns include the stretch from the dam to Cachuma Bay, the dam toward the middle of the lake and the runs near Santa Cruz Bay and Arrowhead Island.

"They typically use three to four colors," Mangler said.

The key to fishing Cachuma is getting out on the water early before the notorious winds that whip through the San Marcos Pass blow you off the water.

While fish can still be caught on breezy afternoons, most of the catches come during the early morning and evening hours. If conditions are really calm in the evening, try turning to topwater baits or shallow-running crankbaits.

Cachuma bass like to feed in the shallows when the conditions are calm and baitfish and frogs come out of hiding.

In the morning, stick to spinnerbaits or crankbaits off rocky points.

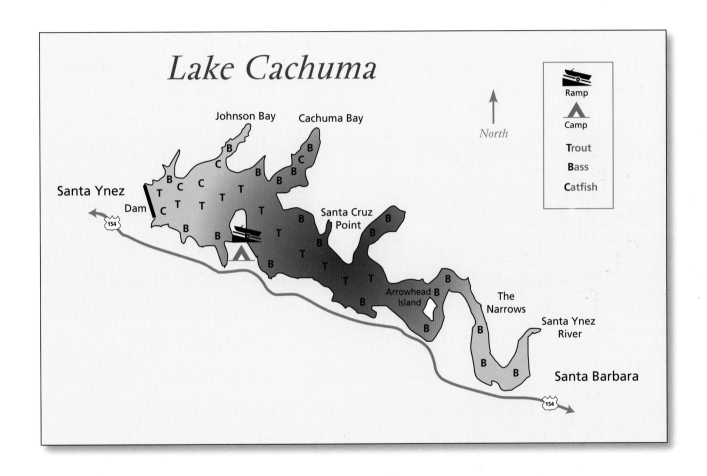

California Aqueduct

Many anglers aren't aware this Golden State channel is open to fishing

Anglers catch everything from stripers to catfish in fishable sections of the California Aqueduct.

Believe it or not, you can fish the California Aqueduct near Taft in the heart of the valley. Anglers regularly catch quality stripers and catfish during the late spring and early summer when pumps push water down the canal.

"When there's water, it's still cooking out there," said Pete Cormier of Bob's Bait Bucket. "Guys have been using mostly lug worms and blood worms for stripers."

The best striper fishing is down near the Buena Vista Golf Course, but that's also the stretch of the canal that receives the most fishing pressure.

"If you can get in there, that's where the fish are," Cormier said. "There's always been good fishing there. There were people who were catching 100 fish a day there for a while."

Lures tempt the bigger fish from 10 to 20 pounds, but most fish run in the 1- to 5-pound range. Catch and release is always recommended in areas that receive as much pressure as the aqueduct, but if you must take fish keep in mind the minimum length restrictions of 18 inches. There is a two fish limit.

Catfish can be had on the standard anchovies, shad, chicken liver and night crawlers. Expect whiskerfish to reach 5 pounds.

Lake Casitas

A favorite getaway for trophy bass hunters

Lake Casitas is known for big bass and is also a decent trout fishery.

Big trout equal bigger bass. That's the formula lake officials have used to turn this 2,700-acre lake into a top-notch bass fishery.

Lake Casitas officials have done a great job in recent years to stabilize its trout fishery and it has benefited both trout and bass anglers alike.

There are regular Department of Fish and Game plants as well as the occasional Calaveras and Idaho trout plants with fish normally checking in at a pound apiece.

Trout anglers usually turn to trolling for rainbows. It is not uncommon for trollers to fish seven colors of lead core (70 yards), taking limits of fish in the 2-pound class on Needlefish in deeper water. The stretch near the dam is another top spot.

The bass bite can flip off and on like a light switch depending on the weather. Warm weather typically means a good bite. Cold weather usually puts the bass bite on hold.

Getting to Casitas

From Ventura, take the 33 Freeway toward Ojai for 10 miles before turning left on Highway 150 for three miles. Turn left on Santa Ana Road and continue to the lake.

In good conditions, bass from 6 to 8 pounds can be caught on trout and crawfish imitations. There are bigger bass in the lake thanks to a resident rainbow trout population that provides plenty of meals for lunker largemouth.

In fact, the lake record is 21.19 pounds, a little shy of the 70-year-old world record of 22 pounds, 4 ounces, set by George Perry in 1932 in Montgomery, Ga. Ray Easley caught the Casitas record on March 4, 1980, on a live crawfish.

But in recent years, swimbaits are the lure of choice by trophy bass hunters.

These lures, which can cost anywhere between $10–100, are usually 9 to 12 inches long and require dependable tackle. Try an eight-foot rod with a quality conventional-style reel and nothing less than 12-pound test line when searching for trophy bass at Casitas (805) 649-2043.

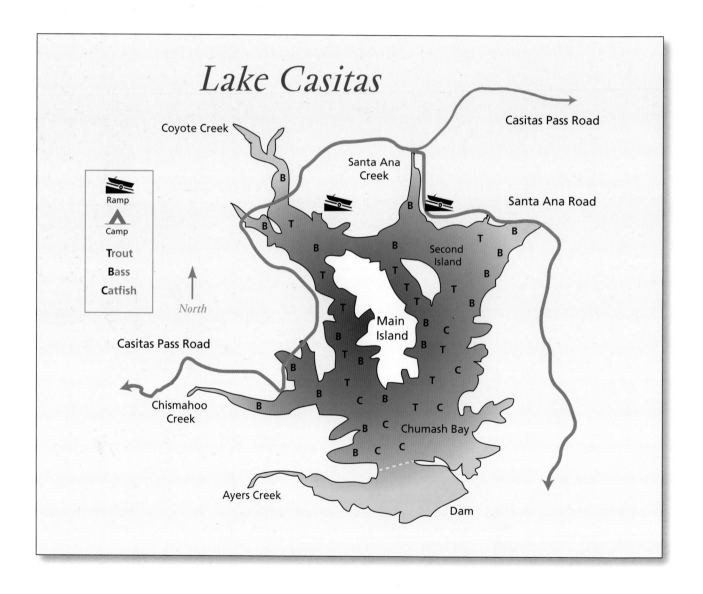

Castaic Lake

Another big bass fishery where trophy hunters roam

The Castaic Lagoon can produce bigger fish than the upper lake these days.

And you thought Casitas had some big bass. Well, a quick look at the world record list shows Castaic Lake has Casitas beat as far as giant bass are concern.

The 2,200-acre lake has kicked out four of the six biggest fish this country has seen—22 pounds, ½ ounce in 1991; 21 pounds, 12 ounces in 1991; 21 pounds, 3½ ounces in 1980; and 21 pounds, ½ ounces in 1990.

The thought of hooking a 20-pound bass makes Castaic one of the most popular lakes on the West Coast. That pressure is also a reason why it hasn't produced a 20-pounder in recent years.

Getting to Castaic

Located about 40 miles north of Los Angeles, Castaic can be reached via Interstate 5. Once you reach Castaic, exit at Lake Hughes Road to reach the lake.

But some Golden State anglers hold out hope there is a world-record fish still lurking the depths of Castaic. For now, the lake record is still Bob Crupi's, set back on March 12, 1991, when he landed a 22-pound behemoth that was just 3½ ounces shy of the world record.

Cottonwood Lakes

The search for gold starts on the upper stretches of Cottonwood Creek

A look at the snow-tipped peaks beyond the first set of Cottonwood Lakes.

Around these parts, anglers eagerly await July 1 like a kid anxiously counting down the days to December 25.

Once July rolls around, every day (at least from July 1 to October 31) feels like Christmas in the Golden Trout Wilderness where heavy concentrations of radiant golden trout race about the depths of the crystal-clear backcountry waters of the Eastern Sierra Nevada.

Reaching golden trout waters is usually no easy task considering most of the alpine lakes and streams that hold them require anglers to horseback in. On average, anglers can expect hikes of four or five miles to find a good golden trout fishery. That's why the Cottonwood Lakes trailhead is such a special destination, offering some of the most convenient access to the state's freshwater fish.

The trailhead is perched higher than 10,000 feet and about 25 miles above downtown Lone Pine—located midway between Reno and Los Angeles along Highway 395. The first Cottonwood Lake can be reached via a 4.5-mile hike that can take anywhere between two and four hours depending on your hiking ability. Once you reach the first lake of the basin you're 11,008 feet above sea level, surrounded by pools and creeks

Getting to Cottonwood

From Lone Pine, take Whitney Portal Road five miles to Horseshoe Meadows Road. Turn left and drive 20 miles to the Cottonwood Lakes trailhead.

brimming with fish that look like they've been sculpted from gold.

Golden trout can be identified by their olive backs, which blend into a blazing crimson lateral stripe and the signature golden belly.

Most of the golden trout in the Cottonwood drainage run in the 7- to 12-inch class. For the record, the state record is 9 pounds, 8 ounces, but don't expect anything bigger than a pound here. Anything over 14 inches is considered a beast in these frigid, nutrient-lacking waters. Keep in mind, the water in the basin was probably snow just a few weeks earlier so it's a good idea to pack some waders.

So what do these fish eat?

Go lakeside on a calm evening or early morning and you'll see exactly what they're after— mosquitoes, mosquitoes, mosquitoes.

The lakes, creeks and moist sections of the trail are plagued by the ravenous insects, so bring plenty of imitations, not to mention repellent and a mosquito mask.

A large Cottonwood golden trout picked up on an Elk Hair Caddis at the first lake.

A wilderness permit from the station is required for camping, and keep in mind that fires are usually not allowed. Check with the tackle shops and ranger station in Lone Pine to determine what the fish are biting prior to your trip. For the most part, anything that resembles a mosquito will probably work.

Start off with a small fly, something in the 14 to 16 range works fine. Try an Elk Hair Caddis, a light Cahill or a Parachute Adams to determine their mood.

Golden trout like this Cottonwood beauty are California's state freshwater fish and there might not be a better place to find them than in the Cottonwood Lakes Wilderness.

If they're not hitting dry flies, try a dry-and-nymph setup. A standard Pheasant Tail trailing a Parachute Adams is a good call in the afternoon when fish feed along the lake bottom and edges. On bright, cloudless days, try switching to streamers and large flies like the Clouser Minnow, Muddler Minnow or Woolly Bugger.

Golden trout aren't easy to catch, so if your luck still doesn't change, you'll need to take another approach. Keep in mind, lake-dwelling goldens naturally prefer to sip up flies off the surface—evident by the rises all over the lake in late evening and early morning hours. If they're not hitting a dry fly, it's time to switch to an emerger or nymph.

A delicate presentation is a must. Try a 5X or finer tippet on a 12-foot leader and stick to subtlety, avoiding drag at all costs. Never jerk the fly and use long, slow retrieves. Unless you're running out of options, it's best to stay away from flashy or bulky patterns that can spook away any whoppers.

Jeff Brackney at Lone Pine Sporting Goods says goldies usually respond well to typical high Sierra patterns such as the Adams, Sierra Bright Dot and the Black Ant.

For the spinning reel anglers, Brackney has just one suggestion.

"Go with something yellow," he said. "A yellow and black (spotted) Panther Martin works great."

Spinners also can use a bubble-and-fly combination with the above patterns. Just be sure to crimp down the barbs on your hooks and stick to flies or artificials at the Cottonwood Lakes. Also note that lakes 1, 2, 3 and 4 are catch and release only. There are five-fish limits at Cottonwood Lakes 5 and 6, which require a six-mile hike and sit at an elevation of 11,186 feet. South Fork, Long, High, and Muir lakes can also be reached from the trailhead.

For the record, Brackney, a local who knows the Golden Trout Wilderness as well as anyone, prefers to get away from it all and fish Cottonwood Lakes 5 and 6.

"I always make sure I get up to Cottonwood No. 5," Brackney said. "I have to be able to keep at least one to eat."

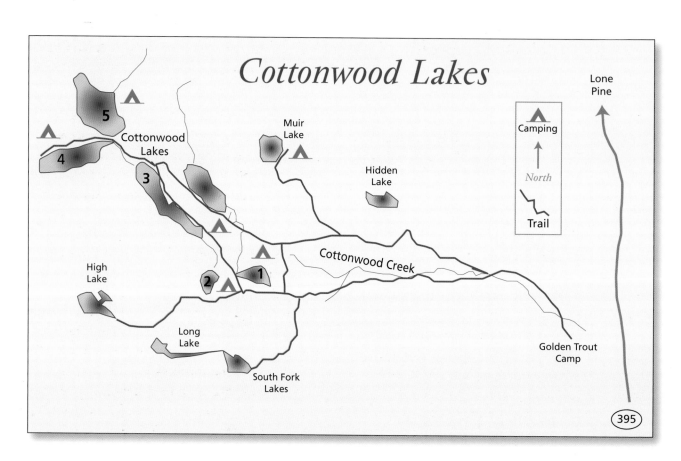

Dinkey Creek

A favorite among Sierra Nevada trout anglers

Brook trout can be caught in the shallows of First Dinkey Lake in the early summer.

It's called the Dinkey Lakes Wilderness, but don't let the name fool you. The Dinkey Lakes Wilderness is more than 30,000 acres of mountain meadows, pines, rocky peaks and gin-clear lakes and creeks.

And the trout in Dinkey are anything but, well, dinky. Its remoteness, mixed with rainbows, brookies and browns are what make this wilderness one of the true gems of the Sierra Nevada Forest.

The Dinkey Lakes Wilderness, at 6,000 feet, stretches across the western slope of the beautiful Sierra and is among the first couple of stops on the forest's main artery, Highway 168.

The wilderness taps into the heart of the forest's diverse geography at Dinkey Creek, located 13 miles outside Shaver Lake. The creek offers a pleasant campground and stretch of river where the pools are filled with rainbows and some wild browns. But don't let your trip end here, the quiet creek is just the beginning.

A dozen miles outside the campground is the Dinkey Lakes trailhead, where the fun really begins for anglers who are willing to do some hiking. For the record, the first lake, Mystery Lake, is about a 2.5-mile trek from the parking lot. Swede, South and the First Dinkey lakes are located within another mile of one another. If you are willing to spend the weekend backpacking along the trail, you can hit seven lakes in a seven-mile stretch (14 miles roundtrip). Just remember to get a permit if you plan on spending the night.

Mystery Lake

The small, shallow lake is the first stop on the trail. Mystery has some hefty resident rainbows, but it's probably the least fished lake with Swede and other larger lakes on the horizon. Despite seeing little fishing pressure, it wouldn't hurt to take a quick breather and chuck a couple of spinners around the perimeter.

Your best bet for a Mystery rainbow is flinging a light-colored Panther Martin or Kastmaster with a quick retrieve to avoid hanging up in the salad below. Fly fishermen traditionally stick to a floating line and a dry-fly approach at this first lake.

Use this rightfully named lake as a test run. If you're catching fish here you're going to have a very productive trip with, say, a possible 50-fish weekend on the horizon.

Dinkey Lakes Breakdown

Mystery Lake: rainbows

Swede Lake: rainbows

South Lake: brookies

First Dinkey Lake: brookies and some rainbows

Second Dinkey Lake and Fingerbowl Lake: both rainbows and brookies

Upper Dinkey Creek: mostly browns with some brookies and bows mixed in

Lower Dinkey Creek: Near the campground, the creek is stocked weekly with bows, but you'll find an occasional brown upstream from the campground and a brookie if you are extremely lucky

Swede Lake

This is where the big, purple-sided rainbows reside. The best fish can be found on the east side of the lake, which holds feisty fish in the deep water that runs up to the granite slopes of Three Sisters Peaks. Because of its depth and size, Swede is a fine spot for belly boaters. If you pack a float

Rainbow trout in the 12- to 14-inch class can be caught at Swede Lake.

Brook trout dominate the catch at the First Dinkey Lake.

tube, make sure to bring your chest-high waders along for the ride because you'll be wading in water that was probably snow a few days earlier.

Most fish cruise the eastern shoreline during the morning and late afternoon hatch. Fly fishermen tend to stick to mosquito imitations. An Elk Hair Caddis is always a good go-to-fly at the lake, and the creek for that matter.

Spincasters can dunk PowerBait or salmon eggs almost anywhere with success. Flipping Super Dupers or Rooster Tails around rocks and other cover along the perimeter is also a sure way to catch 12- to 14-inch fish.

First Dinkey Lake

If you have to pick just one lake to fish, make sure this is it. First Dinkey Lake, with the Three Sisters Peaks providing a jaw-dropping backdrop at 10,619 feet above sea level, is easily the most precious of the dozen or so lakes in the system. And you won't find any genetically altered rainbow trout—born and raised in some Fresno fishery to crave bait—here. There are only gorgeous Dinkey brook trout here, which are spectacular for a number of reasons.

In the late evenings, the mosquitoes come out in full force and the brookies put on a show, make that a ballet, dancing across the surface in search of a hearty meal. It's an incredible sight made more tolerable if you pack plenty of repellent, pants, a long-sleeved shirt and a mosquito mask.

Dinkey Lakes Wilderness

About: A stellar trout fishing and backpacking destination. Along with numerous trails and gorgeous views, the Dinkey Lakes Wilderness is filled with rainbow, brook, and brown trout. Mosquitoes are ever-present.

How to catch 'em: Pack a box full of caddis and your favorite dry flies—anything on the small side works. Anglers can also catch fish on traditional salmon eggs, PowerBait and spinners.

How to get there: From Fresno, take Highway 168 east to the town of Shaver Lake. Turn right at Dinkey Creek Road and continue eastward to the Dinkey Creek recreation area, which offers resorts, campgrounds, picnic areas and plenty of trailheads. The Dinkey Lakes trailhead is located just outside the Dinkey Creek Campground and requires an additional 12-mile drive on a bumpy, dirt road not suited for small cars.

More information: Backpackers are required to obtain a wilderness permit. You can register and find more information at the High Sierra Ranger Station along Highway 168. Call (559) 855-5360 for more information. Be sure to check the weather forecast before making any backpacking trips. Gas and fishing supplies are available at the campground store or in Shaver Lake.

The lively brookies also make good fighting fish, breaking the surface and leaping through the air and spiraling out of control when they finally return to the water. They're not the biggest fish in the wilderness, but if you fish the western portion of the lake near the creek, a colorful 10-inch brook trout shouldn't be too tough to catch.

Ever-present mosquitoes suggest repellent or a head net. Pack a box full of caddis, as the Elk Hair is a must at First Dinkey, although anything on the small side works after about 5 p.m.

Best of the Rest

A basic all-around 5/6-weight fly rod will work fine at Dinkey Creek and the other high Sierra lakes. In the morning and late evening, consider using a floating line for surface action. At the river, or if the midday bite dies down at the lakes, try switching to a fast sinking line to get down to the deeper pockets where the larger bottom huggers hide beneath boulders and fallen trees.

Tapered leaders from 4 to 6X and up to 8 or 10 feet are sufficient. Additional selection patterns that will work in the Dinkey Wilderness include nymphs like the Prince, Pheasant Tail, Hares Ear and Damsel, dries like the Adams, Black Gnat and the Royal Coachman, or streamers such as a Woolly Bugger and Muddler Minnow, an olive and black Matukas or Marabou Leaches.

Spincasters should think small, especially in the creek, which holds little browns throughout. The bigger rainbows can be aggressive but light tackle and 4-pound test on a 6-foot rod should be sufficient.

Stocked rainbow trout and wild browns can be found at Dinkey Creek near the campground.

Isabella Lake

Trout and bass fishing just minutes from Bakersfield

The author with a healthy rainbow caught in one of the coves at Isabella Lake.

With the hard-flowing Kern River pumping in for most of the year, Isabella Lake is often colder than most lakes Central California anglers are used to.

Those cool flows and fast-moving water can put a serious damper on the bass fishing, according to Pete Cormier of Bob's Bait Bucket. So when the bass bite cools off, Cormier and other local anglers switch to crappie and trout.

"When the lake is cold like that, don't expect to catch many bass," Cormier said. "...That's when I switch to crappie."

The bass bite picks up once the weather warms and water levels become more consistent.

A rainbow trout caught near where the Kern River meets with Isabella Lake.

Isabella Lake is a well-rounded fishery home to trout, bass, crappie and catfish.

Getting to Isabella

Take Highway 178 out of Bakersfield east for 45 miles until you reach the lake, which can be accessed from the main road.

Trout fishing is usually good on PowerBait, while catfish are picked up by cutbait anglers fishing the deeper water at the south end of the lake.

Crappies can push 1 to 2 pounds at Isabella. Fish can be found in the shallows near submerged brush, stumps or even docks in 10 to 15 feet of water.

"Minnows and crappie jigs, that's all you need to know," Cormier said. "Use some light tackle and you'll have a blast."

Once you've had your fill at the lake, head up the North Fork of the Kern River where trout to 2 pounds can be had on spinners such as Rooster Tails and Panther Martins.

Both the upper and lower rivers receive plants for most of the year.

Bass can be found on the lower river, hitting Rooster Tails, light-colored crappie jigs or plastic worms.

Kern River

Home to California's state fish along with browns and rainbows

The North Fork of the Kern River is as good a run-and-riffle river as the state has to offer.

The storied history of the Kern River is really a tale of two rivers.

The first, the North Fork, originates in the high Sierra Nevada near Mt. Whitney, plunges through the Inyo and Sequoia national forests and cuts deep into the granite outcroppings that make up the Kern River Canyon. In the spring, snowmelt turns this stretch above the old gold-mining town of Kernville into a fast-moving torrent that's considered one of the most popular whitewater rafting runs in the state.

The second, the South Fork, is a free-flowing river that winds through open meadows and provides habitat for a native species of golden trout.

The two rivers, added by congress to the National Wild & Scenic Rivers System in 1987, merge below Kernville to create Isabella Reservoir and the Lower Kern River. Here, the river carves its way through Sequoia National Park for another 32 miles before finally leaving the canyon to provide nourishment for the San Joaquin Valley.

In the end, the mighty Kern pirouettes through some 60-plus miles of very accessible water that, for the most part, provides the trout-deprived Central Valley with a stellar fishery all year long. Consider the Kern in the early spring when most of the high-altitude rivers look like runs of chocolate milk due to the runoff that swells them to the point where they're almost unfishable.

North Fork

The North Fork of the Kern River, the most popular stretch in the eyes of trout anglers, has gone through some tough times the past few years.

During the summer of 2002, the McNally Fire charred more than 150,000 acres of wilderness and riverfront land in the region north of Kernville. To make matters worse, a massive rainstorm that same year pummeled parts of the Kern River drainage, flooding the river and demolishing the banks of the North Fork.

Today, much of that vegetation along the river's edge has healed and so has the trout population, according to Kernville Hatchery manager Greg Kollenborn. Kollenborn and his staff have helped that cause by stocking more than 100,000 fish in the river. The Department of Fish and Game plants the section above Kernville with mostly half-pound rainbows. In addition, the hatchery has established a trophy trout program that stocks another 4,000 3- to 5-pounders.

"We cover the entire roadside—some 50 miles," Kollenborn said. "But our main stocks stick primarily to the upper river above Isabella Lake, from Kernville to Brush Creek."

Getting to the Kern

From the 99 in Bakersfield, head east on Highway 178 to the entrance of Kern River Canyon. Access is available at various turnouts along the 40-mile stretch up to Isabella Lake. The upper portions of the north fork of the Kern River can be accessed via Kern River Highway.

There's no denying the fire and flooding have changed the path of the river in some areas, forcing the locals to relearn the river's runs. For example, the flood hit the river so hard it altered the streambed in some places, uncovering boulders and digging up new gravel beds. And the fire added to the alteration by singeing the landscape so badly it still feeds silt and sediment into the system after a good rain.

"The sediment has changed some things," Kollenborn admitted. "The river has changed, but it's not necessarily a negative thing. You might not be able to fish the same hole you used to, but the fish are still going to be in there."

A true Kern River Rainbow caught on the upper stretches of the North Fork.

Healthy juvenile brown trout in the Kern's feeder creeks show the system is in good shape.

Guy Jeans, owner and main guide for the Kern River Fly Fishing Guide Service (866) FISH-876, says he's noticed a few shifts in the river's path and also agrees he enjoys the challenge of an evolving river. He says new sediment helps bring new grasses and vegetation to the sandbank, resurrecting the insect life along the river.

That's why he prefers to fish the North Fork, focusing most of his time on the section located just a couple miles north of his fly shop (if there's a closed sign in the window you know where to find him).

"I just love that stretch because of all the pockets and pools, riffles and runs," he said. "There are some big fish holding there, and you can get an occasional brown. In March and April, there's no one here, so the fishing is always good."

That depends on the amount of rain and runoff, of course. If the current is too strong, or if floating debris is present, Jeans cautions to leave the North Fork to the rafters and kayakers and move to the South Fork or the Lower Kern.

But if conditions are calm, he won't hesitate to fish the infamous "Thunder Run" stretch, a Class IV-V run that rafters enjoy because it holds some of the deepest drops the state has to offer. It also holds trophy trout all year long. Trout that can be enticed by nymphs such as pheasant tails and other bead heads. Jeans suggests bringing along some of his homemade emergers, stimulators, various caddis and Parachute Adams.

The North Fork above Isabella offers 25 miles of excellent access along Kern River Highway from Kernville all the way up to Johnsondale Bridge, located east of Johnsondale. Along with holdover trout from Isabella, the lower stretches of the North Fork are stocked throughout most of the year (sometimes on a weekly basis). Some top destinations include the campgrounds at Hospital Flat, Gold Ledge, Corral Creek, Limestone and at

One of the Kern's stocked rainbows.

the power plant. Jeans also recommends tackling the run behind Kernville Park.

"If it doesn't run off, there's also a serious stonefly hatch," he said of the early spring season. "Before the runoff, I'll go down behind the golf course there and catch some of the big holdovers that come up from the lake. If it gets too swollen, it's time to move on."

South Fork and Lower Kern

While the South Fork isn't as likely to swell up as the North Fork, it definitely isn't as angler friendly. In fact, much of the southern portion is only accessible to the dedicated outdoorsmen who are willing to ride in by horseback. But for those who make the trip, catching a golden trout, the state's freshwater fish, is worth the effort.

"That's pretty special upstream," Kollenborn said. "There are no hindrances. No dams to speak of. Just the natural flow of the river and native species."

The Golden Trout Wilderness is typically open to fishing from late April to mid-November. Only artificial lures and barbless hooks may be used.

"It's incredible up there," Jeans said. "I'd compare it to fishing in Alaska. There are big browns and Kern River rainbows. It's totally different up there because the water stays cold all year long. The water could be 56 degrees there in July."

The Lower Kern, on the other hand, is just the opposite. Flows from the lower river are largely dependent on releases from Isabella dam. Portions of the river are diverted to generate power at a trio of hydroelectric facilities and water temperatures can soar to 70 degrees. So the river is far from wild, but it gives anglers a reliable flow for much of the year.

In the spring, the Lower Kern gives fly fishermen a chance at some feisty smallmouth bass. The lower stretches also produce largemouth, catfish, suckers, and planter trout.

"It's a unique river because there are so many varieties of fish in there," said Clay Rutledge of Bob's Bait Bucket in Bakersfield. "There are always a lot of holdover fish because it doesn't get fished as heavy outside of summer. It's not like the Sacramento River where people are lined up shoulder to shoulder. The fish are very catchable down there. You're rarely going to hear of someone not getting their limit."

The Kern River is a fun run-and-riffle water above and below Isabella Lake.

Special regulations are in place on the North Fork where this native rainbow was caught and released.

Another reason the Lower Kern is a favorite among Bakersfield anglers is the location. The entrance to the Kern River Canyon is located just minutes east of Bakersfield along Highway 178, making it a favorite summer destination for the Central Valley and Southern California anglers.

"You could head to the lower river and be fishing in 30 minutes, easy," Rutledge added. "That's the nice part. You don't have to go all the way up to catch fish."

The lower river carries trout from the dam down to the mouth of the canyon but is typically only stocked from the lake to Democrat Hot Springs. Bait anglers suggest fishing scented baits in protected pools along with worms, crickets or salmon eggs. Largemouth and smallmouth regularly track light, brightly colored Rooster Tails, worms, crawfish and crickets just below the lake. And while Kern regulars are hesitant about giving away their secret spots, limits can usually be found at Democrat, Hobo and Sandy flats.

Fly fishermen, who resort to nymphing the cool, slower-moving water below the Edison Flume Power Plant, can limit out in the early spring. Turn to dry flies in the evening if a hatch is present.

Additional Regulations

Anglers should keep DFG regulations in mind when fishing any portion of the Kern River. It is recommended that anglers regularly check the latest regulations before fishing this unique and prized fishery.

On the lower river, and on the North Fork from Isabella Lake to the Johnsondale Bridge, regulations are usually pretty standard with fishing open all year and a daily bag and possession limit of five per day and 10 in possession.

From Johnsondale Bridge on up, the regulations can get a bit trickier. From the bridge to where the U.S. Forest Service Trail 33E30 heads east to join the Rincon Trail, the season runs from late April to mid-November, with a minimum length of 14 inches. Only artificial lures and flies with barbless hooks are permitted. Daily bag and possession limit is reduced to two fish. Winter fishing is catch and release only.

From the Rincon Trail to the mouth of the Tyndall Creek, the summer season is the same although two rainbows that are 10 inches or bigger may be kept here. Conservation-minded anglers, however, encourage fishermen to practice catch and release on these protected runs in hopes of allowing the trout population to succeed.

Searching for Gold

The South Fork of the Kern River is where our state fish calls home.

Although golden trout have been transplanted to lakes and streams from Mt. Whitney to Alpine County, the majestic fish are native to the high country Kern River watershed.

Reaching the true stomping grounds of our stately trout is no simple task as nearly all the streams and creeks that hold them require anglers to backpack or horseback in. On average, the quest for gold is going to take you on a trek of more than five miles, through the oxygen-thin Sierra Nevada air and elevations exceeding 8,000 feet.

"If you can't stand being on a horse for five hours, this isn't for you," advised Jeans, of the Kern River Fly Fishing Guide Service. "But a lot of people are willing to go for it. Even guys who haven't fly-fished before. Then we get up there and their first fish is a golden. Talk about an awesome feeling."

A golden trout caught in the Golden Trout Wilderness.

For those who haven't been lucky enough to catch one of these golden beauties (the season runs from late April to mid-November), these radiant fish have an amazing color scheme that begins with an olive back that blends into a blazing crimson lateral stripe and golden belly that rivals the hue of any other freshwater fish in North America.

On top of their beauty, these little fish can fight. And when you finally land one, you'll be surprised at their size. Don't be discouraged if most goldens run from 7 to 12 inches long. The state record is over 9 pounds, but don't expect to set any records here.

Anything over 14 inches earns bragging rights in these frigid, nutrient-lacking waters.

So when you're stuffing your backpack for your next trip to the South Fork, pack light. A four- or five-piece pack rod with an ultra light spinning or fly reel should be sufficient.

Fly fishermen should contact local guides for up-to-the-minute reports and fly patterns. But don't be scared to tie all your flies before your trip. The resident fish of the south arm aren't too selective because the remote stretch sees very little pressure. Most dry flies, when presented in a cautious, delicate manner, will draw strikes up and down the river.

"They definitely aren't that picky," Jeans concludes. "Flip a dry fly in there and they go after it like a piranha."

Start off with a small fly, something in the No. 14 range works well on a calm morning or evening. Try an Elk Hair Caddis, a light Cahill or Parachute Adams to determine their mood.

If they're not hitting the dries, switch to a nymph setup. A standard Pheasant Tail nymph dangling below a Parachute Adams, as an indicator, is a good call in the afternoon when fish aren't rising on a regular basis.

On bright, cloudless days, try switching to streamers and big flies like the Clouser Minnow, Muddler Minnow or Woolly Bugger. Remember to debarb all hooks and practice catch and release.

When the flows calm in the late summer, the Kern is an ideal fishery for man and his best friend.

Kern River Smallies

All fly fishermen need to know to catch Kern River smallmouth bass is how to grip it and strip it.

Bronzeback fishing on the lower river below the Isabella dam is so simple even amateur fly-rodders can have a field day. All it takes is an olive or black Woolly Bugger, a delicate cast, sinking fly line and a simple cross-and-pull-back retrieve to entice these spirited smallies.

Once there's a fish on, you'll know it's a smallmouth by the way it fights.

"They're fun to catch and they're really superb fighters," notes Rutledge of Bob's Bait Bucket in Bakersfield (661) 833-8657.

For spincasters, Rutledge recommends white or yellow Rooster Tails or small, light-colored plastic worms in the 2- to 3-inch range. Small crappie jigs can also work when fished near cover and submerged logs or boulders in the warmer, sun-drenched pools. If bait is your thing, drop-shot night crawlers, crawfish and crickets will produce decent results in the spring.

Planter trout stick to the cool pools on the lower river.

Kings River

A solid fishery whether it's warm or cold

One of the many pools located along the upper stretches of the wild Kings River.

Rain or shine, frost or drought, the Kings River usually stands up to all of Mother Nature's extremes, especially on the lower stretches.

"The Lower Kings has been good," said Dan Busby at Buz Buszek Fly Shop (559) 734-1151 in Visalia. "The lower portion of the river doesn't get affected by weather. It actually gets better as the fall goes on while the Upper Kings gets blown out."

The most popular stretches are traditionally the stocked runs at Winton Park (below Piedra), Choinumni Park (above Piedra) and near the dam where cold flows hold trout all year long.

Local spincasters have fishing below Pine Flat Dam down to a science, regularly limiting out on casting bubbles trailed with nymphs such as a Pheasant Tail.

Salmon eggs, PowerBait and pink Panther Martins will work in the morning and early evenings, but if the fish aren't biting it might be a good time to turn to a fly.

Fly fishermen say the best time to fling a fly on the Lower Kings is from November to April when the irrigation season dies down.

Getting to the Kings

Take Highway 180 east out of Fresno and follow Trimmer Springs Road toward Pine Flat. The lower river below the dam is a popular spot for anglers searching for planted rainbow trout.

The river can often see very low flows which may dictate fishing dries. When the river is running deeply enough nymphing is a good option during the day until the evening hatch occurs.

Busby recommends attractor patterns size 12–16 and dries such as a Parachute Adams and an Elk Hair Caddis, and urges fly guys to stay away from October Caddis.

Royal Wulffs, Light Cahills, Casanova Caddis and Blue-Winged Olives are good backup flies, according to locals.

"You never know when the hatch comes off," Busby said, "so it's good to have a little bit of everything in a bunch of sizes."

PMDs, Adams, emergers, black ants and olive Woolly Buggers come into play when the trout are really selective, or if there are drastic changes in the weather.

Fly fishermen who want to go the extra mile can fish from Kirch Flat Campground all the way up to Garlic Falls.

Work protected pools with nymphs in these catch-and-release flows beyond Pine Flat Reservoir.

Flows on the upper stretches of the wild Kings River can remain fairly high during the summer.

Lopez Lake

Beat the wind and lunker bass await

A husky double-digit largemouth bass caught and released at Lopez.

This Arroyo Grande lake can be the best lake San Luis Obispo County has to offer. One issue, however, is the wind factor.

Get out to the lake early if you want to beat the breeze and take advantage of this solid, year-round bass fishery. From late morning to late afternoon, frequent thermal winds can turn Lopez into a windsurfer's paradise and an angler's worst nightmare.

The largemouth bite is typically rated "good" by the lake staff, with crankbaits producing consistent results, while drop-shotting plastic worms in the morning and chucking topwater lures in the evening are productive options. The bigger fish are caught off rocky points and deep creek dropoffs in the coves. Big bass can also be caught down by the dam on Rat-L-Traps, MS Slammer lures, jerk baits, and buzzbaits.

Smaller bass can be caught by shore anglers with fish showing near cover and around brushy shoreline. Small crankbaits, Kastmasters and Rooster Tails fool shallow-water bass.

Getting to Lopez

From the 101 in Arroyo Grande, take the Highway 227 exit and follow the signs to the lake, which is located about 10 miles outside of town.

But there's more than just bass in Lopez (805) 489-1006 for store and marina.

The lake also hosts the Lopez Lake Reel 'em In Trout Derby and has a good panfish bite.

Catching tagged trout during the derby can pay big dividends. Just ask Paige Siller of San Luis Obispo, who caught a tagged trout worth $3,000 when she was just 9.

The bluegill, redear and crappie bites also can be rewarding for Lopez anglers. When bass catches slow during the spawn, many boat fishermen turn to panfish, especially crappies, which typically spawn later than bass.

Float tubing is another option for anglers in search of suspended crappies. Try bouncing light-colored jigs, worms or crickets in 15 to 20 feet of water for crappie that range from 10–12 inches.

If you're fishing with a lure or crappie jig, ranger Bob Yetter recommends topping your hook with PowerBait Crappie Nibbles or Eagle Claw Nitro Gems.

Not to be overlooked is a decent bluegill and redear bite in the late spring and summer. Average-sized fish can be picked up by shore anglers and fish surpassing the 1-pound mark can be pulled from deeper water by float tubers and boat-bound fishermen.

Typical outfits for Lopez panfishers include light spinning gear with 4- to 6-pound test line, slip bobbers and night crawler pieces. For pie-pan bluegill, fish close to dropoffs and ledges with 2-inch chunks of night crawlers or an entire mealworm if you've got it.

"Mealworms are always the big bait," Yetter concludes.

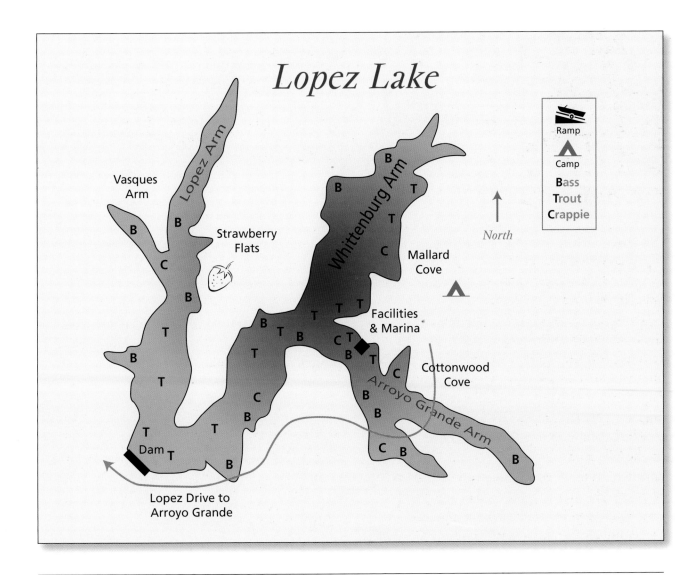

Matilija Creek

Conservation groups are hoping this steelhead water runs free again

A stealthy approach is key when fishing for skittish trout on this small creek.

It's only a matter of time before Matilija Creek runs wild again.

In late 2005, Trout Unlimited, California Trout and San Diego Trout had secured close to $1 million in government grants to remove two dams in the southern portion of the state—Rindge Dam near Malibu and Matilija Dam near Ojai.

Central Coast conservation groups hope the removal of Matilija Dam will allow the southern steelhead, which could access the Matilija from where the North Fork joins Ventura River, to reach backcountry-spawning grounds in the Matilija and other tributaries.

According to local conservation groups, the watershed provides some of the best remaining habitat for the endangered fish and was a temporary home for more than 5,000 migrating steelhead before the 200-foot high dam was built for flood control and water storage in 1948.

With the dam in place, few fish make the trip to the lower portions of the Matilija—located off Highway 33 north of Ojai along Matilija Road. Once the dam is removed, new regulations that resemble those of other coastal creeks in the region will be put in place. Check local regulations for up-to-date information.

Because artificial lures are the rule on steelhead waters, barbless spoons are the best options.

Some good fly patterns include Bunny Leeches, Marabou Flies, Egg Sucking Leeches and egg patterns in red, orange, yellow, or blue.

Merced River

Often overlooked, the Merced adds to Yosemite's unparalleled beauty

Just look at it, sitting there so peacefully. Nobody around to take away from its serenity. The Merced River (you thought we were talking about Half Dome?) is a forgotten treasure lost in the granite faces and waterfalls that dominate the landscape of Yosemite National Park.

Nearly 4 million people travel through Yosemite's majestic valley each year, but rarely do the visitors take notice of the Merced River—arguably the most overlooked river this state has to offer.

"It's pretty remarkable how many people speed right past," said Tim Hutchins of Yosemite Fly Fishing (209) 379-2746. "They come to Yosemite for the sights, not the fishing."

Not that one could blame slack-jawed tourists for stumbling over the river to gawk at the overpowering presence of Half Dome, or the majestic beauty of Bridal Veil Falls. That's how it's always been for the Merced River.

The merciless river, its habitat and wildlife, have been trampled upon since the early 1800s when Spanish explorers first named the river. Early settlers called it El Río de Nuestra Señora de la Merced—River of Our Lady of Mercy. They eventually channeled its untamed flows, blasted its glacial moraine to drop the water table and diverted the river to help quench the thirst of a growing country.

Even then, the Merced was a magnificent river, originating in the high country of the Clark and Cathedral ranges, plunging over Nevada and Vernal Falls and winding its way through the valley, Merced Canyon, and into the parched San Joaquin Valley.

In 1987, recognizing the Merced's significance, Congress designated its upper reaches as a National Wild and Scenic River. Restoration efforts have included replanting vegetation, fencing, and eliminating fish stocking in the park, helping to return the river to a more natural state.

As the sun sets on the valley, sunlight reflects off the face of Half Dome and is mirrored in the Merced River below.

Anglers should use caution when fishing the Merced when it's at its highest flows.

Modern Day Merced

Today, the upper stretches of the Merced and the Kings are designated Wild and Scenic rivers. There's no logging, no mining, no dams, and no cattle grazing—just miles and miles of special-regulation water.

"It's amazing that a roadside river like this can stay in such great shape," said Hutchins, who guides out of El Portal.

"It's not a secret any more. People know the park has some pretty good fishing. It's just not a great place for spin fishermen and it gets pretty rugged in parts, so it comes down to knowing where all the good spots are."

As far as the good spots are concerned, the locals are pretty tight lipped about their favorite stretches. But after some serious prodding, Hutchins will let you in on a couple of his secret holes.

Hutchins, whose El Portal home overlooks some of his favorite runs, knows the Merced about as well as anyone. He's lived near its banks for more than 20 years now and is active in a handful of restoration projects aimed at preserving its beauty.

Some of his favorite drifts are right there off Highway 140, just before the Arch Rock entrance to the park, like the pools across from the El Portal Market, or the runs down by the government service center.

And if you saw the size of the German browns perusing those calm pools in the fall, when the water levels are at their lowest, you'd understand why El Portal is also referred to as "Montana in Your Own Backyard."

Getting to the Merced

The Merced River parallels Highway 140 before the western boundary and Arch Rock Entrance to Yosemite National Park (outside El Portal). The South Fork can best be reached near Wawona along Highway 41 near the South Entrance to the main park.

Rules and Regulations

To keep that stretch feeling like Big Sky Country, the Department of Fish and Game manages the area with special regulations. While fishing is open year-round from the western boundary of the park to Foresta Bridge, only artificial lures and flies with barbless hooks are allowed. No wild rainbow trout may be kept and there is a limit of five browns a day and 10 in possession.

"Everything's wild," Hutchins said. "Nowhere in the park is stocked, so you could have five species of wild trout to chose from. And the park is a big place, so if you don't like the conditions at one part of the river, you can hop in the car and drive another half hour and you're up 5,000 feet higher and enjoying a totally different experience."

The Merced is stocked from Foresta Bridge downstream to Lake McClure, where rainbows are planted on a regular basis and fishing is open year-round. Anglers can fish with bait or artificial lures here, but limits vary throughout the year. From late April to mid-November, anglers can keep five trout. The limit drops to two rainbow trout from mid-November to April.

In the park, the season usually picks up from the final Saturday in April and runs through November 15 and is catch and release only for native rainbow trout.

Because stockings have been stopped in the park, the wild rainbow, brown and brook trout are smaller and harder to come by. That's why many of the region's anglers tend to fish at the lower elevations.

But if you know the right people, you'll come to know the right fishing spots within the park's boundaries.

"I've fished a lot of rivers that I'd never set foot in with a fishing guide," admits Graham Hubner, head fly fishing guide at Southern Yosemite Mountain Guides (800) 231-4575. "Most of the time I think, 'This is a piece of cake. I don't need a guide for this.' But not at the Merced. That river is a mystery. You might see a run and think it's chock-full of fish and not catch one there all day. It's a very finicky river, but it can be a blue ribbon one if you know when and where to fish."

Hubner guides in Southern Yosemite, spending a good amount of time on the South Fork of the Merced, and he admits his favorite part about fishing there is the view.

"There are many reasons why I love fishing here, but foremost has to be the setting," he said. "There's really a great mixture available for you in the 15 or so miles I fish."

The Evening Hatch

While different guides tackle their favorites runs with different approaches, there are at least two things they all seem to agree on. If you're going to fish the River of Mercy, use extreme caution, especially while wading, as the flows can be dangerous when runoff swells the river, and do the majority of your trout fishing in the evening.

The Merced River roars on the upper stretches early in the summer.

A Merced brown cought in the park.

Sightsee all day if you must, but reserve the last couple of hours of the day for taking in some spectacular trout, because when the sun begins to set on Yosemite, the wild rainbows and German browns start their rise.

That's when the hatch begins and the cooling, but still crisp, evening air is filled with so many insects your fly rod doubles as a flyswatter. In the summer and early fall, the dragonflies often become so thick you'll smack one every five minutes or so.

"When you see the dragonflies and the other aquatic insects come around, that's a pretty good indicator that you don't want to pack up and go home," Hutchins said. "It's a great dry-fly river year-round. I'll outfish nymphs with dry flies all the time, which is very unusual."

The Merced is a fly fisherman's paradise, with nearly every favorite bug in the box hatching at one time or another.

When the flows pick up, guides stay away from the Merced gorge and fish the calmer stretches below El Portal where trout will take typical dry flies that resemble any sort of caddis.

While Hutchins recommends staying away from midges in cold water, he does suggest PMDs if fish are rising. Golden Stoneflies will catch fish in water that's 36 degrees because there are so many big, heavy stoneflies on the river.

Along the South Fork, different Mayfly hatches start to come off as the spring runoff recedes with the most accessible runs located in Wawona. Here, Hubner echoes Hutchin's take from further downstream, noting a PMD in the evening is his go-to fly all the way through summer.

"It's the first real good hatch of the season," he said. "I'll fish a PMD in early June into late July. And always in the evening. I don't know why, but the bugs don't seem to come off early in the day. But in the evening, they wake the fish right up."

Even more overlooked than the trout angling at the Merced is the smallmouth bass fishing. While the upper river from the park boundary down to Briceburg is fairly quiet in the morning on into the afternoon, the smallmouth fishing below Briceburg is just heating up. From June through September, the warm water temperatures turn these fish into heavyweight fighters for fly and spin fishermen alike.

Hutchins recommends fishing in the mornings and early afternoons with a black Woolly Bugger or leech look-a-likes. He adds a sinking line and a cross-and-pull-back retrieve can yield "a 50-fish day if the conditions are right."

Once noon comes around, head back up to the park for a scenic picnic before finishing off the day with some stellar trout fishing in El Portal, where wild rainbows range from 12 to 16 inches and the German browns can push 20 inches.

"I swear, every bug I've known in my life comes off at some point in the season there," Hubner concludes. "It's just a phenomenal place and unique in the sense that you can fish for smallmouth in the morning and trout in the evening. What a great fishery, and it will continue to be a great one if people continue to respect it."

Additional Info

Regulations: Special catch and release regulations are in place for native trout from Happy Isles downstream to Foresta Bridge. Anglers here may only use artificial lures or flies with barbless hooks as bait fishing is prohibited.

Best bets: The dry-fly fishing is typically better at the lower elevations in the evening. Successful spots for wild rainbow trout and German browns are located along Highway 140 in El Portal. The smallmouth bite is best in the morning below Briceburg on black Woolly Buggers.

Nacimiento Lake

Spotted, white and largemouth bass will keep you busy at Naci

Good numbers of white bass can help boost catch rates during the spring at Nacimiento Lake.

Ever have one of those days when you've caught so many fish you lose count?

That's what it can be like at Nacimiento Lake thanks to its large population of bass.

Spotted, white and largemouth bass are dispersed throughout the lake, which is located outside of Paso Robles.

The white bass are everywhere after they finish spawning in the Nacimiento River in the spring. The whites usually take over The Narrows, where anglers can reel in dozens of fish on minnows and light-colored Rooster Tails. Whites will convene in Las Tablas Cove where white and yellow spinners and small crankbaits can connect with fish. Just look for the boils and run a spinner or streamer through the strike zone at a constant speed.

Then there's the spotted-bass bite.

"If you can't catch spotted bass (in the spring), you shouldn't be fishing," says marina manager Bob Mooney (805) 238-1056.

During my first-ever trip to Nacimiento, it took an entire two casts before I hooked up with my first spotted bass. I was fishing from the shore in the mid-afternoon as pleasure boats roared past but the spots were still smashing my Rooster Tails.

Getting to Naci

From the 101 in Paso Robles, take the 24th Street/Road G-14 exit and drive 17 miles west on G-14/Nacimiento Lake Drive to the lake.

Your best bet for spots is to focus on rocky shorelines and coves down near the dam. For those who aren't familiar with spotted bass, you also can identify these little scrappy fish by their bright orange eyes and distinct patch of teeth on their tongue.

Although they rarely exceed three pounds, spots can fight like a small but pesky largemouth and are often mistaken for them because of their similar colorations. The main difference in the markings is the spots on the back above the dark lateral line.

A Nacimiento spotted bass, easily identified by its orange eye and spots above the lateral line.

When searching for spotted bass, look for the clear, rocky flows that run in from creeks and small tributaries. They also seem to prefer structure along rocky inlets. If you find submerged brush, logs or heavy cover, you're going to have fun, whether you're throwing spinners, night crawlers, small crankbaits, plastic worms or jigs.

Looking for something different? Try a little spring training for that trout trip you've planned for the Sierra Nevada this summer. Try dusting off the old fly rod and head down to Nacimiento where the spotted bass make a perfect trout substitute.

Try tossing white and yellow streamers and Woolly Buggers and you could be back in the fly fishing mood in a hurry.

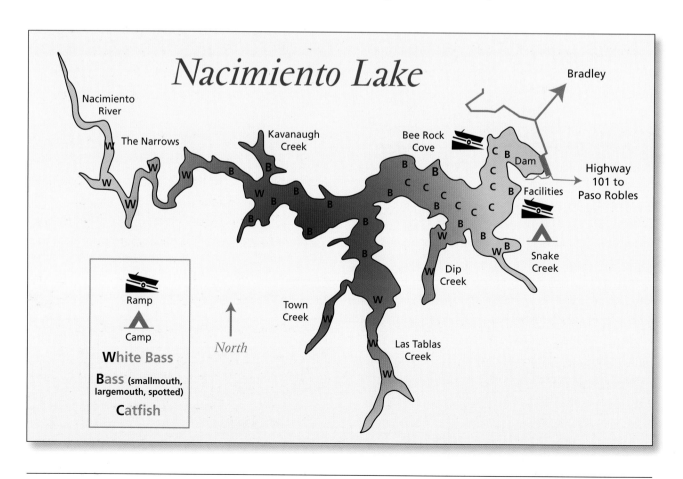

Nacimiento River

Camp Roberts—not what you would expect from an army base

A Camp Roberts tank, nicknamed the "Widowmaker," along a dirt road that parallels the river.

It doesn't exactly look like the best place in the world to cast a fly, but don't let the armed soldiers, army tanks and random explosions off in the distance fool you.

Camp Roberts, located midway between Los Angeles and San Francisco on the border of Monterey and San Luis Obispo counties, is home to one of the only regularly stocked rivers the San Luis Obispo area has to offer. Look past the bunkers, barbed wire and that tank nicknamed the "Widowmaker," and you'll find the Nacimiento River at Camp Roberts is an extraordinary fishery where the rainbows can be found all season long.

The old military post can also make for some stellar turkey, dove, quail, waterfowl, pig, rabbit and buck deer hunts for weekend warriors.

There are some limitations when it comes to fishing on what is currently a national guard training post (call 805-238-8167 for additional information):

- It's only open to anglers on weekends and some holidays from late April to October.
- There's an annual fee of $15 for the season.
- Fishing is only permitted from Gate 3 to the Twin Bridges.
- The post may be closed on short notice for military activities.

But once your waders hit the water, the National Guard goings-ons take a distant backseat to dancing fish, tiptoeing whitetail, bantering beavers and even an occasional bald eagle gliding overhead.

Getting to Roberts

The Nacimiento River is accessible via Camp Roberts on most weekends during the season. Take the 101 about 12 miles north of Paso Robles. Exit west at the East Garrison exit to the Gate 3 wildlife check station. Schedules, maps and fishing forms are available at the gate. Call (805) 238-8167.

History Lesson

Camp Roberts lies on the flat and once-fertile juncture of the Nacimiento and Salinas rivers. A land that was originally inhabited by the Chumash and Salinan Indian nations, which hunted, fished and collected in the region until Spanish explorers arrived in the 1760s.

By 1797 the Spanish had taken hold of the area and extended the old Mission Trail—also known as El Camino Real or the "King's Highway"—with the construction of Mission San Miguel Arcangel. The mission would go on to become one of the most prosperous along the trail, which is said to pass through the camp along Bee Rock Road.

The land changed hands numerous times following Mexico's independence from Spain and when the U.S. took control after California was admitted to the union in 1850.

Nearly 90 years later and with World War II looming, construction of the Camp Nacimiento Replacement Training Center began. The name of the camp was later renamed in honor of Harold W. Roberts, a tank driver who died trying to save a wounded gunner during the war. The post had a pair of training centers and served as a compound for Italian and German POWs during 1941–45.

The training facility was commissioned again in 1950 under the command of the Seventh Armored Division to prepare the state's 40th Division Infantry and artillery units for the Korean War. By the end of the conflict, 300,000 soldiers had passed through the 43,000-acre site.

Camp Roberts was closed in 1970 and a year later it was given to the National Guard as a reserve training center. Today, the camp is still used as a National Guard training post, although training is at a minimum when the post is open to anglers and hunters.

Although rare, white bass provide the best fights on the Nacimiento River at Camp Roberts.

The Nacimiento River at Camp Roberts can be a great place of solitude in the afternoon.

Hot Spots

The Nacimiento, a class I-III river that runs from Fort Hunter Liggett to Turtle Creek, is a slow-moving stream with few deep pools. Flows are still cold and swift despite depths of two to five feet in the spring and early summer, so waders are a good idea. Gravel and sandy bottoms provide a good wade-and-walk opportunity for much of the river.

Some of the most popular stretches of the river are some of the easiest to locate. The first is above High Water Bridge, located near check-in Gate No. 3. About a mile upstream, southwest of the entrance, the Low Water Bridge provides deeper pools for bigger fish and attracts a good chunk of the anglers as well.

Travel a couple of miles upstream and you'll run into the Twin Bridges, where the Department of Fish and Game makes most of its plants. Fishing pressure is greatest here, but get downstream and you'll stumble upon riffles that are as gentle and genuine as they were for the Chumash. The only difference is the eight- to 12-inch rainbows that are planted there every two to three weeks.

In 2004, trout plants were cut by a third because of state budget woes, but there were still plenty of fish to go around, including lunkers left over from the previous season, along with the occasional sucker, carp and squawfish.

If you prefer to catch trout, you may want to stick to fly fishing at Camp Roberts.

Caught on the Fly

The prized fish at Camp Roberts has to be holdover rainbow trout that have been in the system a year or two. These beautifully colored fish have dark olive tops with sides a shade of bright pink or crimson.

Some productive flies for these older fish stem from the Adams family, which has been catching trout across the country since before the post was born. There are countless variations and adaptations that work at this fishery, although the go-to fly is the Parachute Adams. Try a pink-topped hi-viz parachute with a beadhead nymph of some sort dangling a couple feet below depending on the water and flow levels.

Nacimiento rainbows, like many Golden State river trout, prefer cooler temperatures and a healthy supply of oxygen and food. Take time to survey the rapids, runs, riffles and pools. Bigger fish seem to hide out under shaded banks or near structure such as rocks, vegetation, tree roots and logs.

Protective pockets are sure to hold hearty survivors that have been turning up their snouts at PowerBait and salmon eggs all season. The bad news? These lies can present all sorts of problems for fly fishermen.

The bottom line is a stealthy approach when hunting for these very wary trophies. Position yourself so you can cast and drift drag-free for as long as possible. And don't cast directly into a trout's strike zone, or you'll spook the fish.

Looking for something more than trout? Fling streamers for a shot at a rare bass. Nacimiento River is one of the only rivers in the state that produces an occasional smallmouth, largemouth, white and striped bass.

The white and striped bass will provide the best fight and can be picked up in some of the deeper pools located upstream on purple or black Woolly Buggers.

Stripers, white bass and "wiper" hybrids are rare on the upper stretches of the Nacimiento River.

Planter rainbow trout are the most common catches at the Nacimiento River.

The Best of the Rest

Most of the fish pulled out of the Nacimiento River come on the usual spinners, salmon eggs and various colors and flavors of PowerBait.

Camp Roberts trout fall for the standard spinners, salmon eggs and dough bait.

Another solid bait is Uncle Josh's cheese-flavored trout bait, which works well in pools protected from the current.

If you're looking for a wildcard bait, toss a night crawler or a mealworm. Worms can entice anything from a two-pound sucker to a two-foot squawfish. Anglers in search of carp can have a blast at Camp Roberts, if they take the right approach. Like most carp, Nacimiento River carp are picky eaters and easily spooked.

The good news? Nacimiento Reservoir, which feeds into the river, is known to carry some of the biggest carp in the state. In 1968 at the lake, Lee Bryant caught the state record, a 52-pound carp.

You won't pull any state records out of the river, but whether you're in search of holdover rainbows or football-sized carp, Camp Roberts has a little something for everyone.

Not bad for an old military post.

Pine Flat Reservoir

Home to a healthy population of spotted bass

Spotted bass seem to prefer cool, rock-bottom mountain waters like Pine Flat Reservoir.

Pine Flat Reservoir not only keeps the Kings River in check, it produces state record spotted bass as well.

This always-evolving reservoir was created in 1954 with the completion of the Pine Flat Dam, whose initial purpose was providing flood control, regulating irrigation water, and providing hydroelectricity in the process.

It turns out this late-blooming fishery, located at an elevation of 1,000 feet in the Sierra Nevada foothills outside of Fresno, is a stellar spotted bass fishery as well.

In fact, Brian Shishido landed the state record on this water in a bass tournament during the 2001 spring season. Shishido hit the 10-pound,

4-ounce hog throwing a Senko on just 8-pound test line. As Shishido proved, finesse fishing is the key to finding good numbers of spotted bass at Pine Flat as many anglers downsize to 8- or even 6-pound test line.

Getting to Pine Flat

From Fresno, head east to the Kings River Canyon on Highway 180 for about 18 miles. Take a left on North Piedra Road and continue for 8 miles before making a right on Elwood Road. Make a left on Pine Flat Road at 2 miles.

Pine Flat Reservoir

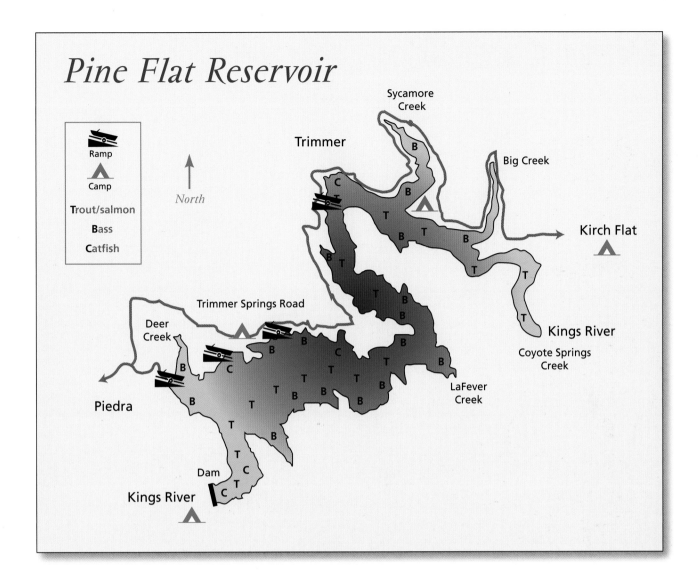

Ramp
Camp
Trout/salmon
Bass
Catfish

North

Sycamore Creek

Trimmer

Big Creek

Kirch Flat

Trimmer Springs Road

Deer Creek

Piedra

Kings River

Coyote Springs Creek

LaFever Creek

Dam

Kings River

No one is quite sure why the spotted bass at Pine Flat are a bit larger, but it's likely in part to solid shad and crawfish populations in the lake—not to mention plenty of other species, including smallmouth and largemouth bass, catfish, sunfish, crappies, trout and even salmon.

For bass, plastics in shad and crawfish patterns are popular. Bunches of bass, mostly spots, can be found around concentrations of shad trapped in coves or creek channels and around rock piles or other cover. Drop-shotting plastic worms will also work around the rainy season when night crawlers are being washed into the river and reservoir.

Trollers will run into the occasional rainbow trout and a few land-locked salmon with Rapalas and Needlefish down to 2 or 3 colors, depending on water temperatures. The dam area is a popular spot for cold-water species, as is the run in front of LaFever Creek and the Trimmer Marina.

Shore fishermen often follow the same approach used by anglers fishing the Kings River below the dam, fishing with a spinning-reel outfit tipped with a casting bubble and fly. Most anglers will stick with bead-head nymphs about 36 to 48 inches below the bobber.

Piru Creek

A fine trout fishery located less than an hour from downtown Los Angeles

Piru Creek's water levels depend heavily on the flows out of nearby Pyramid Lake.

At times, Piru Creek is flourishing as one of the best tailwater fisheries this side of the Sierra Nevada.

Other times, Piru is in serious pain.

One problem is water levels are dependent on nearby Pyramid Lake, which at times lets out flows that measure as little as two cubic feet per second and as much as 40 cubic feet per second. The two extremes are both harmful and detrimental to the stream's resident trout and aquatic life.

Then, there's its proximity to the Los Angeles area. Located less than an hour from downtown, Piru sees as much pressure as any fishery in Central and Southern California. And with that pressure come two more harmful p-words: poaching and pollution.

Getting to Piru Creek

Take Interstate 5 about 15 miles north of Santa Clarita. Take the Templin Highway exit and go west and then north on Golden State Highway to the parking area next to Piru Creek. An Adventure Pass, available through local retailers, is required to park in the lot.

That's why it is important for anglers to abide by the rules and regulations when fishing precious wild trout streams like Piru.

On the creek and its tributaries upstream from Pyramid Lake, only artificial lures with barbless hooks may be used. There is also a two-trout limit on this section of the stream.

From Pyramid Dam downstream to the bridge approximately 300 yards below Pyramid Lake, the river is closed to fishing all year.

From the bridge to the falls about a half-mile above the old Highway 99 bridge, fishing is open year-round but only artificial lures with barbless

hooks may be used and all fish must be released unharmed.

Anglers must also remember to pack out everything they pack into the wilderness and display a Los Padres Forest Adventure Pass on their vehicles. An adventure pass can be picked up at nearby sporting good stores.

Spinners such as Panther Martins, Mepps, and Rooster Tails are really the best two options for spin-cast anglers.

Fly fishermen turn to caddis, Tricos, or PMDs and switch to stoneflies in the colder months.

Piru Creek can see low flows in the late summer.

Lake Piru

Lake Piru often gets overlooked because it's located so close to a number of stellar fisheries, including Piru Creek and Castaic Lake and Lagoon.

The lake also gets overlooked because it isn't known as a trophy bass fishery. Sure, there are largemouth on hand, but the best bite at Piru is usually for rainbow trout.

Boat anglers typically troll for trout near the dam and south end of the lake in 30-plus feet of water. Needlefish and large Rooster Tails are the top baits with most fish running in the 1- to 2-pound class.

Getting to Piru

From Interstate 5 near Valencia, exit Highway 126 toward Piru. In Piru exit north on Main Street and continue to the lake on Piru Canyon Road.

The sunfish bite can be decent in cover around Piru's perimeter. Anglers from boats and shore can score panfish on small jigs.

Most of the bass hit small plastics, worms, and even crickets for anglers intent on catching a largemouth.

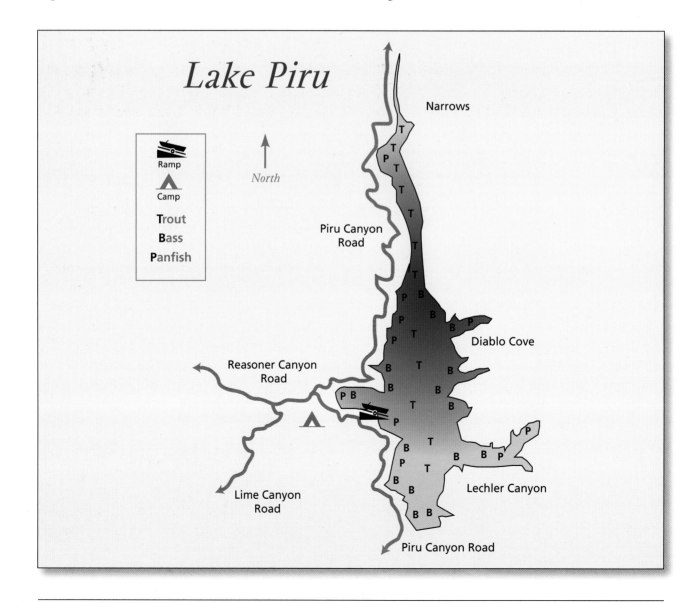

Pyramid Lake

Once a fishery in ruins, this lake is slowly inching back from disaster

Striped bass are the top draw at Pyramid Lake, located right off Interstate 5.

On March 23, 2005, this was a Pyramid in ruins.

Pyramid Lake, once an impressive striped, largemouth and smallmouth bass fishery located off Interstate 5 in Gorman, was an icky black mess after an estimated 126,000 gallons of crude oil spilled into the lake when a rain-induced landslide ruptured a high-pressure oil pipeline in the steep vicinity of Posey Canyon.

While officials weren't concerned about potential contamination of the region's drinking water, they were worried about threats to wildlife. The Department of Fish and Game continues to monitor the biological effects of the spill.

Some local anglers, however, believe catch rates have plummeted since the spill, noting that fishermen heading out to Pyramid can expect bass catches to be down and smaller than in previous years.

In the meantime, fishing for trout might be your best bet as long as the DFG continues consistent plants.

It's also worth noting the lake's resident striped bass, like coastal steelhead trout, are one of the most resilient species the state has to offer. Some hefty liners still reside in the lake, so pack plenty of trout imitations for your trip along with an extra spool of heavy or braided line.

Only time will tell if the lake can bounce all the way back from one of the worst ecological disasters this region has seen.

Getting to Pyramid

About 20 miles north of Valencia, Pyramid Lake is located just west of Interstate 5. Take the Smokey Bear Road exit to get to the lake.

Salinas River

One of the few north-flowing waters out west and a fragile steelhead passageway

The Salinas River, when it's flowing, is an oddity in that it is one of the few north-flowing rivers in the United States.

The Salinas River is not only the largest river in the Central Coast region, it's also the most mysterious.

The seasonal river is an oddity in that it flows underground for much of the year. It's even stranger in that it's a north-flowing river, one of the few out west, joining the likes of the San Joaquin, Snake, Big Horn, Gallatin and Yellowstone rivers.

The Salinas, which usually runs dry above ground by the summer or early fall, stretches

Getting to the Salinas

The Salinas River, which runs from central San Luis Obispo County to Moss Landing in Monterey Bay, is accessible via public trails in Santa Margarita, Atascadero, Paso Robles, Bradley, King City, Soledad and Monterey where the river runs through Salinas River State Park and meets up with the Old Salinas River and Elkhorn Slough before dumping into Monterey Bay.

some 155 miles in San Luis Obispo and Monterey counties, connecting the heavily-farmed Salinas Valley with the coastal range and Monterey Bay.

The southern end of this seasonal steelhead fishery begins in the La Panza Range east of the City of San Luis Obispo and flows north to Santa Margarita Lake, a result of a dam placed on the river between the small towns of Pozo and Santa Margarita.

Below the small but popular bass, trout and crappie haven that is Santa Margarita Lake, the Salinas follows the 101 freeway past Atascadero and Paso Robles where it meets up with the tail end of two of its largest tributaries, the Nacimiento and Santa Antonio rivers. Farther north, the fast-flowing Arroyo Seco River dumps into the Salinas near Greenfield.

Because it receives runoff from these three unique rivers, two of which drain from the bass-heavy reservoirs, the Salinas is home to numerous warmwater species, including white, spotted, largemouth and striped bass originating from Nacimiento and San Antonio lakes. Anglers should note the fishing season on the Nacimiento River is different from that of the Salinas and is typically only accessible via Camp Roberts during the general trout season because the river runs on government property.

Steelhead and wild trout also call the Salinas home for portions of the year. Steelhead are willing to swim 100 miles or more from Monterey Bay to

An unnamed tributary of the Salinas River.

A wild trout caught near where a Salinas tributary dumps into the main Salinas River.

the southern gravel-bottom spawning grounds of the Arroyo Seco and nearby feeder creeks.

The river meets Monterey Bay just south of Moss Landing where it meets with the Old Salinas River and Elkhorn Slough before dumping into the Pacific Ocean. The river used to flow directly into the bay to the south, but its original course changed as a result of the 1906 earthquake.

Because it is an annual steelhead passageway, the Salinas is only open to fishing during the standard steelhead season from December-March on Saturday, Sunday and Wednesdays along with legal holidays and closing day. The Salinas is a special-regulation water with a zero limit for steelhead. Only barbless, single hooks may be used on artificial lures or flies. No bait is permitted.

Bass, sunfish, carp, Sacramento suckers and squawfish make up most of the catches at the Salinas, unless you stick to fly fishing.

Fish the deeper pools under bridges and overpasses and around submerged structure for trout. There are few trees directly along the Salinas River's banks on the southern stretches, but if you find a brush-covered bank, trout can be found below the sheltered dropoffs and overhanging vegetation.

For the most part, fishing on the Salinas is a challenge unless you're at the right place at the right time. The key is to keep moving until you locate a place where fish may stack up.

Good all-around flies for the Salinas include Muddler Minnows and beadhead Woolly Buggers, which may pick up the occasional bass. Egg patterns are popular on the northern stretches of the river, as are egg-sucking leeches and glo bugs.

Pink or yellow Panther Martins and silver or blue Blue Fox spinners resembling small baitfish are popular lures on the Salinas.

Shrimp flies and crab look-alikes are popular with surf fishermen at the Salinas River Refuge, where anglers can hook up with typical surf species such as surfperch and jacksmelt.

Graves Creek is one of dozens of feeder creeks to the Salinas River.

Lake San Antonio

Plenty of shad means plenty of bass at this often overlooked fishery

The author with a feisty smallmouth caught in a San Antonio cove.

When freshwater anglers think striper fishing, they think Lake Mead or Lake Castaic, not Lake San Antonio.

But an abundance of shad on the lake can be credited to the lake's lunker liners.

"The striper fishing is incredible here," said Jessica Smiley at the Lake San Antonio Marina (805) 472-2818. "There's a lot of activity because of the shad. That's what they've been hitting. You can use a dip net to catch shad for bait in the morning."

The main points on the lake produce big fish all year, including those off of the lake's many small coves including Harris Creek and North Shore campground.

Trollers use shad, anchovies and night crawlers to catch most of the stripers, but experienced anglers know it's a good idea to string up extra rods with topwater plugs in case fish boil at the surface. If you don't have a topwater setup in the wings, the school can be gone before you know it. Trollers also spend their days jigging spoons in 20 to 30 feet of water.

MS Slammers, created by local angler Mike Shaw, have also become a popular big-fish lure around these parts. The plugs are imitations of rainbow trout and kokanee.

No matter your bait of choice, timing is always the key when heading out to San Antonio, located about 25 miles outside Paso Robles. The striper

Getting to San Antonio

The lake is accessed from Paso Robles, Bradley, and Lockwood. The main access is Interlake Road on the west side of the lake that runs from the dam at Nacimiento Lake north to Lockwood. East side access is via Jolon Road, then New Pleyto Road.

bite is better in the early morning, while large and smallmouth bass can be picked up in the shallows a little later. The wind plays a factor during a lull period from noon to 4 p.m. when the crappies take off and bass become active again in the evening.

Night fishing for catfish, and stripers, is also popular because the lake is open to fishing 24 hours. The best place to find catfish—the lake holds both channels and blues—is down around the houseboats or near the dam. Popular baits include anchovies, night crawlers, cut mackerel and shad.

Largemouth bass hit along the banks and rocky points. Nice-sized fish can also be caught in the coves and adjacent to rocky shorelines. Bee Rock and Cemetary coves are your best bests when the wind picks up in the afternoon. Stick to crankbaits, crawfish imitations and split-shotting soft plastics and crankbaits if you're hoping for largemouth bass.

If you're searching for striped bass, patience is the key. It takes some time, but once you get one more could be on the way.

"It comes and it goes as far as the stripers are concerned," said the marina's Ali Lohuis.

Even with the ups and downs of the striper bite, San Antonio is still a popular destination for veteran striper anglers, including regulars from the Bakersfield area.

"San Antonio, that's where everybody goes," said Pete Cormier of Bob's Bait Bucket in Bakersfield.

His response is a bit of a head-scratcher considering Cormier's store is some 140 miles away from the lake.

"It's well worth it," Cormier added. "It doesn't seem that far once you get out there and start catching fish."

San Antonio plays host to regular bass tournaments, including many float tube tourneys. The North Kern Float Tubers and Bass-n-Tubes, out of San Jose, are regulars at the lake. And the tubers agree, early spring is the best time to go tubin' as the pleasure boaters are less frequent with the cooler weather. San Antonio, which has 5,500 surface acres of water and 60 miles of shoreline, is a favorite getaway for water skiers and jet skiers during the late spring and summer.

Earlier in the year, stripers tear up Bucktail jigs and silver swimbaits at the north end of the lake. Catch one in a float tube however and these liners—in the 8- to 20-pound range—could take you for a ride back to Bakersfield.

San Luis Reservoir

San Luis Reservoir is probably best known for kicking out a world record striper back in 1992. Hank Ferguson caught the 67-pound, 8-ounce liner at the O'Neill Forebay to set the landlocked all-tackle record for the species.

But today, most of the liners at the man-made lake are in the 10-pound class. According to Larry Bristow of Lucky Larry's Bait, the best spots for stripers are coves and points such as Goosehead Point.

"I'd suggest fishing all the little coves," he said. "Head down to the deeper water near the dam and fish the coves and along the points down there. The fish are right there around the edges."

No single bait seems to do the trick, more like four or five as the day wears on. Bristow recommends anglers experiment with trolled lures such as a deep-running minnows and Needlefish. Other times cut bait, pile worms and bloodworms have been the best options.

The black bass bite usually heats up with the weather. Bristow suggests plastics and crankbaits such as Rapalas or Rat-L-Traps.

Getting to San Luis

Take Highway 152 west out of Los Banos for about 12 miles to either the San Luis Creek or Basalt boat ramps.

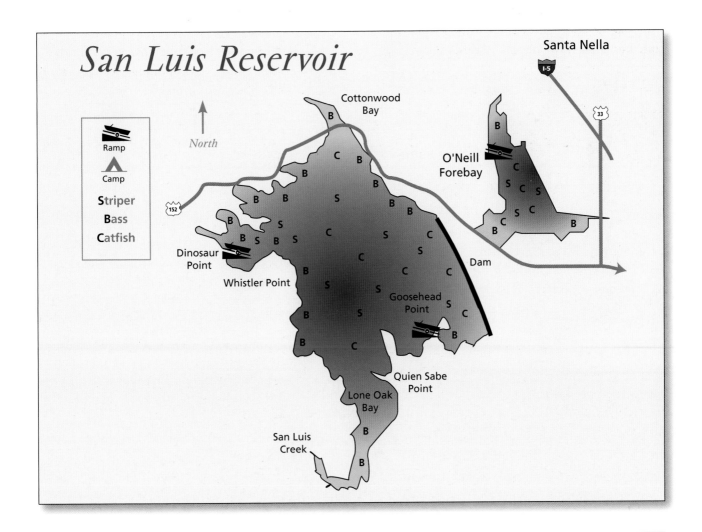

Santa Margarita Lake

Also known as the Salinas Reservoir, "Margaritaville" is healthier than ever

Santa Margarita has bounced back from drought years to become a stellar all-around fishery.

> *"I have spoken of the rich years when the rainfall was plentiful. But there were dry years too, and they put a terror on the valley."*
> —*East of Eden*, by John Steinbeck

John White doesn't remember the last time Santa Margarita Lake looked this healthy.

Crystal-clear water spills over the banks and lush green hills, providing a spectacular spring backdrop. All sorts of wildlife are sprinkled about the lake's edges, and large schools of fish dart about the shallows.

"It's been a long time coming," the local tournament angler says while flippin' a section that had been dry and brown for years. "I don't know if I've ever seen the lake look this good."

In September 2004, Santa Margarita Lake had dropped below 30 percent of its capacity for the first time in more than a decade.

Because Santa Margarita—a major source of drinking water for San Luis Obispo—had been reduced to a puddle, local water managers feared a major drought like those of the late 1980s and early 90s would suck the area dry.

The following season winter and spring showers quenched any drought concerns and

The author with a Santa Margarita largemouth caught off a rocky point on a crankbait.

breathed new life into a fishery anglers are rightfully calling "Margaritaville" again.

Not only was the Salinas Reservoir at full capacity for the first time in seven years (as high as 105 percent in March 2005), but it added a new-and-improved marina store for the first time since 2003 after low water levels deflected a majority of the area's anglers and pleasure boaters to nearby Nacimiento, San Antonio and Lopez lakes.

Don and Sandra Lopez opened a full-service outfit in summer 2005. It includes boat repairs and a handful of rental boats.

Boat anglers have two launch ramps to choose from, which wasn't always the case during the dry spells.

Trout plants were restored and the lake's resident population of largemouth bass, catfish and panfish have all kinds of new habitat.

Getting to Margarita

From the 101 just north of San Luis Obispo, take the Santa Margarita/Highway 58 exit for two miles and turn right onto Pozo Road for eight miles to Santa Margarita Lake Road, which runs to the lake.

The fishing at Santa Margarita is beginning to rival the conditions of the lake's heydays in the mid-'90s and '80s.

"It's seems like everyone's catching everything," said Ranger Chuck Woodard, "Bass, trout, crappie…there's something for everyone."

Trolling for Trout

The trout bite is best before the heat begins beating down on the lake in the summer.

In the spring and early summer, the California Department of Fish and Game stocks as often as every couple of weeks. The lake also receives fish from the Calaveras Trout Farm.

"The trout bite's pretty good on dough baits and spinners," Woodard points out. "During the season there usually are a lot of fish hanging around the marina ramp after plants."

Three or four days after a plant, trout usually head for deeper water. But for the first couple of days, trout can be hauled in on spinners and scented baits.

Shore fishermen stick with ultra-light tackle such as Kastmasters, Rooster Tails, Super Dupers and Panther Martins on 4- to 6-pound test. Bait anglers cast into deeper water with salmon eggs, rainbow PowerBait and night crawlers. Trollers do best on large yellow or white Rooster Tails and Needlefish in The Narrows, the stretch in front of the marina and down near the dam.

Rainbow trout often stack up near feeder creeks and coves around the lake.

Santa Margarita Lake is a solid black crappie fishery.

Schooling Crappies

One day they'll be there in a thick school. The next they're gone.

Santa Margarita's black crappies can be hard to figure out, but once you get a handle on their tendencies the crappie bite here is as good as anywhere in the state.

The key to finding a nice school is seeking out the right temperature and cover. It's no secret slab sides, a warm-water fish, prefer warmer water. That's why float tubers are often the most successful crappie fishermen.

Tubers have an advantage because they can get a better feel for changes in water temperatures as they kick along.

For example, if the lake is hovering around 60–64 degrees, belly boaters will kick until they find a brush-laden cove in the mid to upper 60s. If the inlet is in full sunlight and is protected from the wind, they've found an ideal spot.

Keep dropping crappie jigs, grubs, minnows or night crawlers in and around brush piles and it's only a matter of time before you hit the strike zone.

Flippin' for Bass

When spring comes around, the bass make their seasonal move into the new shallow breaks in search of nesting sites. Some bass spawn earlier in the warmer sections of lake, but for the most part these northern strains are in their prespawn feeding mode.

White, pictured catching a five-pounder in the "sticks," and many tournament anglers in search of quality bass swear by flippin' and pitchin' dark plastics in and around cover with 8-foot rods and 30-pound test. Those seeking good numbers of bass also turn to hard baits in the late afternoon and evenings.

Drop-shotting worms, or tossing spinnerbaits and crawfish look-alikes work while sight fishing during the day, but switching to hard baits once the sun ducks over the hills seems to be the most productive approach.

The best hard baits resemble shad, are slow moving and make plenty of noise. Top shallow-water options include lipless baits like a Rat-L-Trap, Strike King Diamond Shad Premier, Cotton Cordell Super Spot, small-lipped Rapalas such as a Fat Rap, Stanford Cedar Shad or an Abu Garcia Tormentor.

Topwater baits such as poppers, walkers and frogs work well at sunset. And while night fishing is not permitted at Santa Margarita, the ranger staff allows anglers to fish up to 30 minutes after sunset—which is often the best bite of the day.

"Crankbaits have been the best bait around sunset" in the fall, Woodard said. "When there is no moon, it seems like the bass are going crazy for crankbaits and hard baits in the shallows."

Many tournament anglers turn to flippin' and pitchin' for bass.

Santa Margarita is a popular lake for Central California anglers because the shallows are always calm and free of swimmers. The lake, which was created by the damming of the Salinas River, is off limits to jet skiers and swimmers because it is a water source for the City of San Luis Obispo. No bodily contact with the lake is allowed, although float tubing is permitted if no contact with the water takes place.

Because the lake has such unique restrictions and has had adequate rain in recent years, local anglers figure the bass fishery will only continue to improve at "Margaritaville."

"It's been fantastic," White concluded. "You couldn't even launch your boat there a year ago. Now the lake is the best it's looked in years. There's so much cover there it should be a tremendous spawn and the survival rates should be better than ever. It really bodes well for the future of the lake."

Because of its trout population, bass can be tempted by crankbaits off rocky points.

Top-water baits work best in the morning and evening hours.

Additional Species

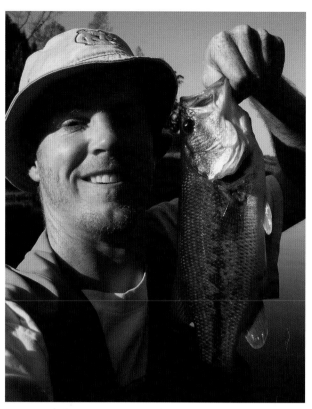

Santa Margarita Lake (805) 788-2397 is also a great getaway for catfish anglers.

Most cats are picked up on stink baits, night crawlers, chicken livers, anchovies, cut bait or mackerel. In the spring, catfish can be picked up in flooded zones near the mouth of the river or the handful of creeks that spill into the coves on the backside of the lake.

But the best time for cats is in the summer and fall seasons when fish congregate down near the dam in the deepest water of the lake. That's where cats to 20 pounds can be picked up. The key is patience and waiting for whiskerfish to track down the bait. If you don't have the patience, better stick to bass fishing. The best catfish anglers are almost always the most patient fishermen as well.

Santa Margarita Lake reached full capacity in 2005 for the first time in seven years.

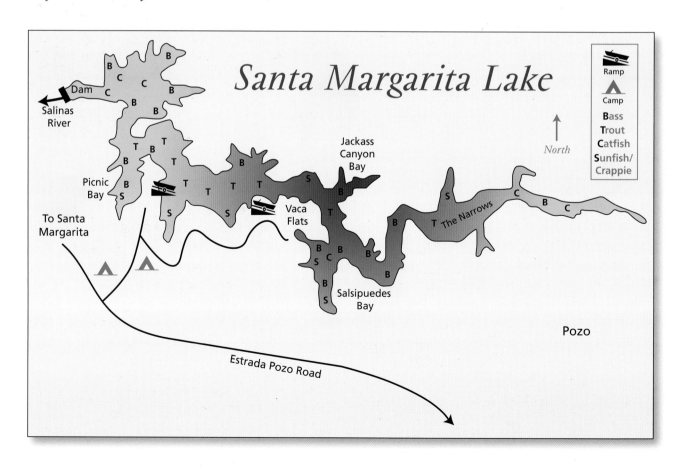

Santa Paula Creek

Santa Paula trout are well worth the hike

The best fishing for wild trout at Santa Paula Creek is above the waterfall.

Look past the local college, avocado farms and oil wells that sour the lower portions of the creek, and you'll see Santa Paula Creek for what it's supposed to be—a historic southern steelhead spawning habitat within the Santa Clara River watershed.

The Department of Fish and Game has halted plants on this tributary of the Santa Clara and is working with the Santa Paula Creek Fish Ladder Authority and other local organizations to help repair damaged fish ladders and provide other restorations that will help improve steelhead passage and habitat in Santa Paula Canyon.

Getting to Santa Paula

Take Highway 126 from Ventura to the town of Santa Paula and take the Highway 150 exit toward Ojai. Take the 150 for about 5 miles to Thomas Aquinas College and park outside the campus entrance gate. Follow the "Trail Hikers" signs to the trailhead, located off the perimeter road that winds counterclockwise around the campus.

Like the Santa Clara's other embattled tributaries, Piru and Sespe creeks, the Santa Paula has been subject to the same stressors that plague the urban watersheds—loss of riparian habitat, streambed alteration caused by flood control structures, habitat fragmentation, and degradation of water quality. All of this makes for difficult fishing on the lower stretches of the creek.

While conservation efforts are taking place, the best fishing on the Santa Paula will be above the falls and tributaries located 3 miles upstream from the Highway 180 bridge.

That makes for a long but mandatory hike along the Santa Paula Creek Trail, scooting past Thomas Aquinas College (a four-year Catholic liberal arts school), ranch houses and the thumpity thump of those rusty old oil wells. After the first mile, the eyesores fall off and the trail follows the creek upstream through the towering Topatopa Mountains of the Los Padres National Forest.

The hike to Santa Paula Canyon Falls is about three miles. Backpackers can stay at Big Cone Camp, located just before the falls. The best fishing on the Santa Paula is above the falls or farther up the East Fork and its feeder creeks.

Tiny nymphs and dry flies are the norm on this small-water stretch. Small, barbless spinners such as pink Panther Martins will also work for these small, wild trout on the upper stretches.

Because there are few trees along the lower stretches of the creek, trout can be very skittish in the afternoon light.

Santa Ynez River

A unique river in northern Santa Barbara County

The Santa Ynez River, located outside of Solvang, provides cool flows into Lake Cachuma.

Outside the self-proclaimed "Danish Capital of America" runs an equally quaint, Old World-type fishery that is as unique as the nearby city of Solvang.

Santa Ynez River is a very distinct stretch of water and once you get a handle on its regulations, it can be a good getaway for Central California anglers.

While the river and its tributaries downstream from Bradbury Dam are closed all year, the river and tributaries upstream from the Gibralter Dam are open to year-round fishing with a bag limit of two trout.

The Santa Ynez River is located in the Santa Ynez Mountains north of Santa Barbara in the Los Padres National Forest.

The river is stocked near the ranger station and campgrounds along Forest Road 5N18.

Because this river is also home to wild rainbow trout, anglers are encouraged to use barbless hooks and practice catch and release.

Small Panther Martins and Rooster Tails are always solid bets on coastal streams like the Santa Ynez for spin fishermen.

Getting to Santa Ynez

From the 101 in Santa Barbara, head north on Highway 154/San Marcos Pass for about 10 miles. Turn right onto Paradise Road NF 5N18, leading to the Santa Ynez River recreation areas and campsites.

Sespe Creek

Known as 'Southern California's last free river'

Sespe Creek is home to a strain of endangered Pacific steelhead.

At first glance, the Sespe Creek Wilderness is far from spectacular.

In a state that's spoiled with breathtaking backcountry trout waters, the Sespe can seem a bit bare and worn down in the eyes of an outsider.

The Sespe, located less than 60 miles outside the Los Angeles area, is indeed the creaky backbone of what is still a very weary wilderness in the Los Padres National Forest. But look at that same stretch of canyon through the eyes of its resilient wildlife and you'll see a different storyline: A tale of resurrection that has breathed new life into a handful of endangered species bouncing back from the brink of extinction.

"Nor do I know of any other water course anywhere that compares with this wild, twisted, rock-walled canyon," condor activist and conservationist Ian McMillian wrote decades ago. "Located, almost in surrealistic fashion, near the northern edge of one of the world's most bizarre metropolitan developments, the crooked Sespe is fantastic beyond anything man has yet constructed."

Called a "dead river" by many Southern California anglers just a few years ago, the highly litigated Sespe and its wilderness are alive again, as are its embattled residents—including the endangered Southern California steelhead, California condor and Arroyo toad.

"I have personally never considered the Sespe dead," said Sespe fly fisherman Matt Coyle. "Hibernating maybe, dead no. The recent wet weather has done what it has to our local streams all across Southern California, rejuvenating them, in some cases, extremely so."

So is the case with Sespe Creek, a 20-minute drive from the quiet town of Ojai in Ventura County. Its watershed stretches some 270 square miles, marrying the coast and transverse ranges together in harmony. Fir and pine trees are sprinkled about the highest slopes, which can reach 7,000 feet. Chaparral dominates the lower elevations with manzanita and sage following the river down to its confluence with the Santa Clara River.

The Sespe Creek Trail is your fishing guide, winding you through one of the best remaining habitats for the Southern California steelhead, believed to be the strain of Pacific steelhead from which all others evolved.

"Sespe Creek and the Ventura river system are probably the last truly viable streams in Southern California for the Southern Steelhead, a genetically different strain from the steelhead found in the northern part of our state," Coyle said. "If we are to return the steelhead to a viable species, it is ultimately the most important piece of water in the state. Steelhead runs in the '30s and '40s were in the tens of thousands. Today, in good water years, steelhead runs are at best in the hundreds. We must protect this waterway if this species is to survive."

The trail—which originates at the parking lot near the old Middle Lion Campground—will wet your feet at times, although waders aren't necessary. In fact, anglers should avoid wading in at-risk steelhead waters such as the Sespe.

Many believe the trout in the Sespe and its tributaries have been adversely affected not only by fire, siltation and erosion, but by foot traffic in the shallows and spawning areas as well. Hiking off trail on the creek's banks can also result in loss of vegetation, which in turn changes the complexion of the creek and causes temperature changes that can negatively impact future spawns.

The wild Sespe is a fun run-and-riffle river.

So instead of trampling new growth, anglers should remain on trail or stick to rock hopping along the creek.

That special care from anglers and hikers, along with the dedicated efforts of activists and organizations such as the local conservation group C.R.E.W. (Concerned Resource and Environmental Workers), had helped the Sespe battle back from the runoff and other complications caused by the Wolf Fire of 2002.

However, the Day Fire in 2006 destroyed even more native vegetation and left a charred landscape that's struggled to hold considerable amounts of water during the rainy season. While the effects on the fishery are unknown at the publication date of this guide, runoff, erosion, and sedimentation are expected to be a major concern in coming years. Keep updated on reports about the area.

A Conservative Approach

Now to get to these gorgeous wild fish, anglers are encouraged to wear quality, broken-in hiking shoes as the trail pushes on all the way down to nearly reach Fillmore.

You don't need to hike all the way down to catch fish, but there are plenty of obstacles along the way—including slippery rocks that anglers will encounter from the onset. That's where dependable hiking shoes, with plenty of traction, come in handy.

The first real obstacle is the initial stream crossing at the beginning of the hike. After that, you may encounter as many as a dozen creek crossings early in the season. The next major crossing is about a couple of miles down the trail.

Once you reach Oak Flat and Willett campgrounds, there are two or three single-track turnoffs that can take you off the beaten path down to the main river. But the best fishing lies downstream past the swimming holes and developed camping sites where most backpackers unwind and set up camp for the night.

Your best bet is to tackle one of the solid runs that follow the Oak Flat and Willett camp areas.

And there are plenty—some can span as long as a football field—to be had as the trail rolls down to its junction with Johnston Ridge and Alder Creek.

If you make it that far, it's time to head back as that portion of the Sespe is closed to fishing

One of the Sespe's resident rainbow trout.

(from Alder Creek to the confluence with Santa Clara River). The Sespe and its tributaries before the Alder confluence are open to fishing year-round, but are catch and release only. Bait is prohibited and only barbless artificial lures or flies may be used.

"It is extremely important to handle any fish caught from the Sespe very gently and with as little stress as possible," Coyle stressed. "Each fish caught has the potential to become a steelhead smolt. This will help put the steelhead back on the map."

What to Bring

Along with quality hiking and backpacking gear, which should include plenty of water or a purifier, anglers will want to pack tons of artificials.

The flashing blade of a small, in-line spinner is as irresistible to native rainbows as they are to planted fish.

Weight-shank spinners such as a tiny Panther Martin, Rooster Tail or Mepps can be productive all day and all season long if fished in the proper manner.

The key is deciphering where the fish are holding.

In the summer, fish tend to avoid shallow stretches in direct sunlight. When fishing late in the season, or during the midday, it's best to search for the deeper pools and fish a spinner slowly enough so that it will reach the bottom dwellers.

A dependable Sespe lure is a yellow, spotted Panther Martin. Fished slowly and steadily, it dives right down to the strike zone.

In the winter, switch to bright, slow-moving lures as fish are holding sluggishly in the colder, deeper pockets. Large white Rooster Tails, silver Kastmasters and Blue Foxes are reliable options when runoff occurs. Add a split shot just above the lure if it isn't sinking deeply enough into the current.

Two spools of fishing line might be a good idea if you don't fish the Sespe often. Bring one spool of 2- or 4-pound test line for when water levels are down and a second with 6 to 8 pounds for when levels are up. To get pinpoint accuracy with each cast, turn to a smooth-casting line such as Berkley's Trilene XL.

Keep in mind, when water levels rise, bigger adult fish might be coming your way, so be prepared with a balanced line that is as strong as it is undetectable.

In the summer, all that's left are fish in the 6- to 10-inch range. Anything bigger would surely earn bragging rights during a summer getaway.

Experienced anglers send most of their casts straight upstream on fast-moving runs, retrieving the lure at a consistent speed that keeps the blades moving and avoids hang-ups. In slow water, cast upstream and across, bringing the lure back diagonally through any hot pockets.

On the Fly

Fly fishermen need to look no further than the shallows to figure out what the resident rainbows are feeding on in the Sespe.

The shallow stretches are sprinkled with minnows, underwater insects and thousands of pollywogs, a major reason why the fish that hang around these parts tug around bass-like potbellies.

That's where nymphs and streamers come in.

The Sespe is a great dry-fly fishery in the late afternoons and evenings. A #14 Elk Hair Caddis or Adams will draw a rise once the sun is off the water. The subsurface bite can last all day.

The key is tying a pattern that directly imitates the above aquatic groups. These flies must look, feel and, most importantly, accomplish a sink rate that will find the correct feeding level.

A Hare's Ear is a classic all-purpose nymph that should produce consistent strikes, especially if it's tied with a larger wing casing near the hook's eye, which can resemble the head of a pollywog. A Pheasant Tail can also be tied in a similar, top-heavy fashion (called the flashback) where the peacock herl that makes up the thorax is covered by Pearl Lurex epoxy.

A Muddler Minnow replicates a Sespe pollywog.

Streamers in the Muddler Minnow family are another reliable option, imitating everything from pollywogs to minnows and small bottom-dwellers of the Sespe.

As you tie, remember to modify your hooks so you don't have to worry about busting off barbs in the middle of a good hatch. And if you're on the water during a hot bite, do the fishery a favor and downsize to a smooth single hook to ease stress on the fish.

Remember, only when you respect a precious fishery like the Sespe will it return the favor.

"Indeed, the Sespe is the wild heart of Southern California, a next-door wilderness where transformation can happen in a heartbeat or a blink of an eye," Bradley John Monsma writes in his book *The Sespe Wild: Southern California's Last Free River* (Reno: University of Nevada Press, 2004). "To consider this place, therefore, is to call up issues crucial wherever wilderness and cities meet: recreational impacts on wildlife habitat, the dynamics of accessibility and protection, the physical and psychological need for healthy ecosystems, threats of development and resource extraction.

"The Sespe—past and present—reminds us that nature and culture have always intermingled."

Shaver Lake

A kokanee paradise tucked away in the Sierra Nevada

Shaver Lake is fishable from spring through fall before the winter snowfall comes.

Troll a Needlefish and you never know what you're going to hook up with at Shaver Lake.

While the rainbow trout and kokanee bites take off in the spring, anglers also have an outside shot at catching a brown or brook trout along the way.

Fishermen hoping for rainbows should troll light-colored Needlefish, gold Kastmasters or spoons near the dam, marina and various creek inlets around the lake. Tunnel Creek and Edison Cove are good spots for soaking bait.

Trollers prefer to hit the stretch of lake between McDonald's Cove and Shaver point or the wide-open stretch before Chipmunk Cove.

Anglers focusing on kokanee should start with Super Hoochies and the various colored spoons and kokanee bugs local shops recommend that day. Pink has been a hot color the past couple of seasons.

Next to your warmest jacket—the wintry reservoir is located at an elevation of 5,370 feet—your best friend at Shaver will be your fish finder.

Determining the depth at which fish are holding is the key. Once you locate fish, limits can be common. Most anglers begin their day fishing at 20 to 30 feet.

Brown trout can be targeted by shore anglers tossing Rapalas, Roster Tails and Kastmasters. Some popular spots include down near the

Getting to Shaver

From the Fresno area, head north on Highway 168 for about 48 miles to the town and lake.

marina, the launch ramp and near the dam. Night crawlers can catch all of the above plus bass. For current conditions, call Shaver Lake Sports (559) 841-2740. As the spring wears on, trollers fall back on four to five colors of lead core line with a 6-foot, 6- to 8-pound leader. Early in the season when the water is still murky, anglers can get away with 10- to 12-pound test line in search of large holdover fish.

White Needlefish and silver Kastmasters are the lures of choice for locals heading out toward Eagle Point and the North Fork of Stevenson Creek.

Shore anglers prefer dunking dough baits and night crawlers down to 20 feet as well. Salmon eggs on light tackle such as 4- to 6-pound test are another option.

Anglers stuck on fishing for bass should toss spinnerbaits or crankbaits off the lake's many rocky points during the morning period.

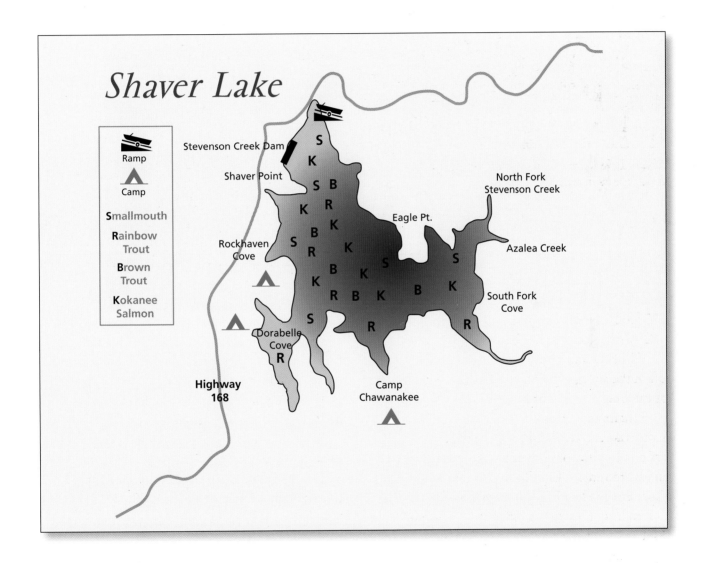

Whale Rock Reservoir

Nothing but landlocked steelhead at this rare fishery

A steelhead enhancement project began at Whale Rock Reservoir in 1992.

When steelhead fishing slows around the state, it's just getting started at Whale Rock Reservoir.

The 590-acre reservoir located in Cayucos is open during the general trout season from 7 a.m. to 4 p.m. Wednesday through Sunday with about two miles of shoreline open to the public. A self-registration booth is set up at the entry gate where anglers can deposit a day use fee of $2 for adults and $1 for children.

According to officials, no more than 300 to 400 fishermen visit the lake each year because boats aren't allowed and bass are nowhere to be found. There's nothing but steelhead here thanks to an enhancement project that began at the reservoir in 1992, offsetting the ecological impact the dam had on Old and Cottontail creeks. Now, landlocked steelhead are around all season long (from late April to November).

While live bait is not allowed, PowerBait or salmon eggs remain a viable option. When traditional baits aren't working, tie on a small, crankbait and shake things up. Big rattlers can produce big results. Hey, they don't call it Whale Rock for nothing.

Getting to Whale Rock

From Highway 1 in Morro Bay head north toward Cayucos and exit right at Old Creek Road. Stay on Old Creek for two miles until you reach the gate on your left.

Resources

With 100 miles of coastline in San Luis Obispo County alone, Central Coast anglers have plenty of fishing spots to uncover. The following resources will help you get the most out of your next fishing trip.

Freshwater Fish Identification Chart

A look at some of the common species in the Central California region

Bluegill

Redear

Green Sunfish

Black Crappie

Sacramento Squawfish or Pikeminnow

Striped Bass

Catfish

Western Sucker

White Bass

Smallmouth Bass

Spotted Bass

Largemouth Bass

Rainbow Trout

Brook Trout

Golden Trout

Brown Trout

Record Watch: Big Fish List

Department of Fish and Game's listing of California all-tackle records

Fish	Angler	Weight	Date	Location	County
Arctic Grayling	Don Acton, Jr.	1 lb. 12 oz.	8/27/74	Lobdell Lake	Mono
Largemouth Bass	Michael Arujo	21 lb.12 oz.	3/5/91	Lake Castaic	Los Angeles
Smallmouth Bass	Tim Brady	9 lb. 1 oz.	3/20/76	Trinity Lake	Trinity
Spotted Bass	Brian Shishido	10 lb. 4 oz.	5/3/01	Pine Flat Reservoir	Fresno
Striped Bass	Hank Ferguson	67 lb. 8 oz.	5/7/92	O'Neill Forebay (San Luis)	Merced
White Bass	Milton Mize	5 lb. 5 oz.	5/8/72	Ferguson Lake	Riverside
Bullhead	Gary Dittenbir	4 lb. 8 oz.	10/7/93	Trinity Lakes	Trinity
Carp	Lee Bryant	52 lb.	4/1968	Nacimiento Reservoir	SLO
Blue Catfish	Roger Rohrbouck	101 lb.	3/12/00	San Vicente Reservoir	San Diego
Channel Catfish	Lee Porter	52 lb. 10 oz.	7/12/93	Santa Ana River Lakes	Orange
Flathead Catfish	Billie Joe Potter	72 lb. 14 oz.	4/22/03	Colorado River	Riverside
White Catfish	James Robinson	22 lb. 0 oz.	3/21/94	William Land Park Pond	Sacramento
Orangemouth Corvina	Dick Van Dam	37 lb. 0 oz.	7/15/88	Salton Sea	Imperial
Black Crappie	Wilma L. Honey	4 lb. 1 oz.	3/29/75	New Hogan Lake	Calaveras
White Crappie	Carol Carlton	4 lb. 8 oz.	4/26/71	Clear Lake	Lake
Sacramento Perch	Jack Johnson	3 lb. 10 oz.	5/22/79	Crowley Lake	Mono
Chinook Salmon	O.H. Lindberg	88 lb.	11/21/79	Sacramento River	Shasta
Coho Salmon	Milton T. Hain	22 lb.	1/3/59	Paper Mill Creek	Marin
Kokanee Salmon	Dick Bournique	4 lb. 13 oz.	8/1/73	Lake Tahoe	Placer
Sargo	Mike Leonte	4 lb. 1 oz.	1972	Salton Sea	Imperial
American Shad	Craig Stillwell	7 lb. 5 oz.	5/9/85	Feather River	Butte
Sturgeon	Joey Pallotta	468 lb.	7/9/83	San Pablo Bay	Contra Costa
Bluegill Sunfish	Davis Buckhanon	3 lb. 8 oz.	7/10/91	Lower Otay Lake	San Diego
Green Sunfish	unknown	1 lb. 12 oz.	6/3/78	private pond near Bella Vista	Shasta
Pumpkinseed Sunfish	Dave Smith	1 lb.	8/4/98	Mt. Meadows Reservoir	Lassen
Redear Sunfish	Anthony White	5 lb. 3 oz.	6/27/94	Folsom So. Canal	Sacramento
Tilapia	Carol A. Bellamy	3 lb. 8 oz.	11/27/00	Palo Verde Canal	Riverside
Brook Trout	Texas Haynes	9 lb. 12 oz.	9/9/32	Silver Lake	Mono
Brown Trout	Danny Stearman	26 lb. 8 oz.	4/30/87	Upper Twin Lake	Mono
Bull Trout	James S. McCloud	9 lb. 11 oz.	5/1968	McCloud Lake	Shasta
Cutthroat Trout	William Pomin	31 lb. 8 oz.	1911	Lake Tahoe	Placer
Golden Trout	O.A. Benefield	9 lb. 8 oz.	8/18/52	Virginia Lake	Fresno
Lake Trout	Robert G. Aronsen	37 lb. 6 oz.	6/21/74	Lake Tahoe	Placer
Steelhead Rainbow Trout	Robert Halley	27 lb. 4 oz.	12/22/76	Smith River	Del Norte
Rainbow Trout	Frank Palmer	27 lb.	10/2/05	Lake Natoma	Sacramento
Warmouth	Russell Jacobs	15 oz.	5/21/04	Hensley Lake	Madera
Mountain Whitefish	Gregg Harris	3 lb. 1 oz.	1/24/04	Lake Tahoe	Placer

GPS Resource: Central Coast Waters

Coastal rivers, creeks and lakes of Monterey, San Luis Obispo, Santa Barbara, Santa Cruz, and Ventura counties

Rod? Check. License? Check. GPS? Check. Yes, GPS (Global Positioning System) units are becoming that important in the eyes of bass pros and recreational anglers alike.

GPS receivers take advantage of satellite technology to determine a user's location, speed and direction among other mapping and tracking functions.

Companies like Garmin and Magellan have taken the technology to a new level, offering units that not only keep you from getting lost, but lead you to that hard-to-find creek and mark your favorite spots for future reference.

Many of the handheld units, such as Garmin's eTrex line, come equipped with fishing and hunting calculators that provide optimal feeding times. Receivers are generally preloaded with basemaps containing general information about popular North American lakes, rivers and roads, and can be loaded with detailed map data (purchased separately) geared toward fishermen and boaters.

A quality handheld GPS receiver usually costs around $150. Many fish finders are also adding GPS capabilities, running anywhere from $500–1,000.

The waters listed on the following pages are not all open to the public, and are listed only as a GPS resource. Enter the latitude and longitude coordinates into your GPS receiver to locate a

GPS units such as Garmin's eTrex Legend contain basemaps complete with lakes, rivers, and roads. They are even preloaded with marine navigation aids.

water and mark the waypoint for future reference. These coordinates may also be entered manually into some Web-based mapping programs, such as Google Earth, for a broader overview of the fishery on your computer.

Many GPS receivers can download maps, tracks and waypoints from computer-based mapping software.

GPS Resource: Central Coast Waters

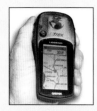

Waters listed are not all open to public but are listed as a GPS resource. Enter the latitude and longitude into your GPS to locate each fishery and save the waypoint for future use to help you better navigate your way about the destination listed.

Monterey County Creeks, Streams, Rivers

Water	Location	Latitude	Longitude
Agua Fria Creek	Jolon	35.898°N	121.239°W
Agua Mala Creek	Carmel Valley	36.438°N	121.626°W
Alder Creek	Villa Creek	35.858°N	121.416°W
Alisal Creek	Salinas	36.687°N	121.640°W
Anderson Creek	Partington Ridge	36.153°N	121.666°W
Anthony Creek	Alder Peak	35.945°N	121.333°W
Basin Creek	Sycamore Flat	36.284°N	121.430°W
Bear Basin Creek	Ventana Cones	36.298°N	121.649°W
Big Creek	Lopez Point	36.070°N	121.599°W
Big Creek	Rana Creek	36.380°N	121.561°W
Big Sand Creek	Sycamore Flat	36.325°N	121.488°W
Big Sandy Creek	San Miguel	35.792°N	120.726°W
Big Sur River	Big Sur	36.281°N	121.858°W
Bixby Creek	Point Sur	36.371°N	121.902°W
Black Rock Creek	Carmel Valley	36.423°N	121.737°W
Blue Creek	Ventana Cones	36.303°N	121.666°W
Boronda Creek	Carmel Valley	36.391°N	121.629°W
Bruce Fork	Ventana Cones	36.349°N	121.650°W
Buck Creek	Partington Ridge	36.135°N	121.648°W
Los Bueyes Creek	Jolon	35.877°N	121.230°W
Burns Creek	Partington Ridge	36.141°N	121.654°W
Los Burros Creek	Burnett Peak	35.874°N	121.218°W
Cachagua Creek	Carmel Valley	36.402°N	121.659°W
Calaboose Creek	Sycamore Flat	36.296°N	121.494°W
Camp Creek	Zigzag Creek	36.197°N	121.576°W
Carmel River	Monterey	36.536°N	121.927°W
Carrizo Creek	Cone Peak	36.092°N	121.432°W
Chalone Creek	Greenfield	36.348°N	121.210°W
Charley Creek	Priest Valley	36.133°N	120.711°W
Charley Creek	Priest Valley	36.133°N	120.711°W
Chris Flood Creek	Burro Mountain	35.784°N	121.271°W
Chualar Creek	Chualar	36.571°N	121.539°W
Chupines Creek	Carmel Valley	36.453°N	121.695°W
Church Creek	Zigzag Creek	36.243°N	121.568°W
Cienega Creek	Partington Ridge	36.244°N	121.655°W
Comings Creek	Big Sur	36.332°N	121.755°W
Conejo Creek	Rana Creek	36.391°N	121.593°W
Copperhead Creek	Bryson	35.870°N	121.007°W
Cottonwood Creek	Cholame Valley	35.804°N	120.340°W
Cow Creek	Monarch Peak	36.181°N	120.801°W
Danish Creek	Ventana Cones	36.372°N	121.663°W
Deer Creek	Williams Hill	35.889°N	121.059°W
Dolores Creek	Ventana Cones	36.251°N	121.692°W
Doolans Hole Creek	Ventana Cones	36.265°N	121.744°W
Doud Creek	Soberanes Point	36.422°N	121.914°W
Dutra Creek	Burro Mountain	35.800°N	121.283°W
Dutra Creek	Burro Mountain	35.801°N	121.283°W
East-North Fork Lewis River	San Benito Mountain	36.254°N	120.715°W
Elkhorn Slough	Moss Landing	36.806°N	121.789°W
Estrada Creek	Burro Mountain	35.773°N	121.274°W
Finch Creek	Rana Creek	36.391°N	121.593°W
Forest Creek	Bear Canyon	36.067°N	121.312°W
Gabilan Creek	Jolon	35.892°N	121.221°W
Gabilan Creek	Salinas	36.687°N	121.640°W
Garrapata Creek	Soberanes Point	36.418°N	121.915°W
Gibson Creek	Monterey	36.506°N	121.938°W
Gulch House Creek	Bryson	35.789°N	121.093°W
Hames Creek	Wunpost	35.878°N	120.833°W
Harper Creek	Spreckels	36.580°N	121.717°W
Harris Creek	Tierra Redonda Mtn.	35.813°N	120.927°W
Higgins Creek	Zigzag Creek	36.158°N	121.559°W
Horse Creek	Sycamore Flat	36.253°N	121.415°W
Horse Run	Junipero Serra Peak	36.233°N	121.454°W
Jackson Creek	Big Sur	36.326°N	121.768°W
Jacques Hanlon Creek	Mount Harlan	36.649°N	121.458°W
James Creek	Rana Creek	36.389°N	121.593°W
Johnson Creek	Gonzales	36.517°N	121.442°W
Jolon Creek	Jolon	35.939°N	121.165°W
Joshua Creek	Soberanes Point	36.416°N	121.904°W
Juan Hiquera Creek	Big Sur	36.263°N	121.799°W
Kirk Creek	Cape San Martin	35.988°N	121.495°W
Las Gazas Creek	Carmel Valley	36.492°N	121.750°W
Launtz Creek	Big Sur	36.309°N	121.791°W
Lime Creek	Lopez Point OE W	36.120°N	121.631°W
Limekiln Creek	Chualar	36.525°N	121.516°W
Limekiln Creek	Lopez Point	36.009°N	121.519°W
Lion Creek	Ventana Cones	36.252°N	121.694°W
Little Burros Creek	Burro Mountain	35.863°N	121.269°W
Little Cholame Creek	Parkfield	35.909°N	120.436°W
Little Sand Creek	Sycamore Flat	36.336°N	121.498°W
Little Sur River	Point Sur	36.335°N	121.892°W
Logwood Creek	Partington Ridge	36.249°N	121.717°W
Lost Valley Creek	Zigzag Creek	36.169°N	121.514°W
Malpaso Creek	Soberanes Point	36.481°N	121.937°W
McCoy Creek	Palo Escrito Peak	36.493°N	121.383°W
McWay Creek	Partington Ridge	36.158°N	121.671°W
Middle Fork	Ranchito Canyon	35.859°N	120.599°W
Mill Creek	Cape San Martin	35.983°N	121.491°W
Mill Creek	Big Sur	36.371°N	121.843°W
Miller Fork Carmel River	Ventana Cones	36.354°N	121.650°W
Mission Creek	Bear Canyon	36.011°N	121.253°W
Mocho Creek	Partington Ridge	36.227°N	121.659°W
Monroe Creek	Greenfield	36.270°N	121.180°W
Moro Cojo Slough	Moss Landing	36.803°N	121.784°W
Mud Creek	Villa Creek	35.864°N	121.432°W
Mud Creek	San Juan Bautista	36.782°N	121.585°W
Muddy Creek	Gonzales	36.603°N	121.406°W
Mule Canyon Creek	Pfeiffer Point	36.222°N	121.761°W
Murry Creek	Jolon	35.971°N	121.171°W
Nacimiento River	Bradley	35.832°N	120.755°W
Natividad Creek	Salinas	36.687°N	121.640°W
Negro Fork	Cape San Martin	35.997°N	121.381°W
Negro Fork Nacimiento River	Cape San Martin	35.998°N	121.381°W
Nelson Creek	Smith Mountain	36.017°N	120.590°W
North Fork Big Creek	Lopez Point	36.099°N	121.577°W
North Fork Big Sur River	Partington Ridge	36.244°N	121.679°W
North Fork Los Burros Creek	Alder Peak	35.876°N	121.293°W
North Fork San Antonio River	Cone Peak	36.065°N	121.387°W
North Fork San Jose Creek	Monterey	36.519°N	121.908°W
North Fork Willow Creek	Cape San Martin	35.903°N	121.417°W
Paloma Creek	Sycamore Flat	36.273°N	121.449°W
Pancho Rico Creek	San Ardo	36.016°N	120.911°W
Parsons Creek	Gonzales	36.603°N	121.425°W

Water	Location	Latitude	Longitude
Partington Creek	Partington Ridge	36.176°N	121.695°W
Pfeffer-Redwood Creek	Big Sur	36.251°N	121.786°W
Pheneger Creek	Big Sur	36.269°N	121.807°W
Pick Creek	Partington Ridge	36.210°N	121.633°W
Pinal Creek	Cone Peak	36.080°N	121.395°W
Pinalito Creek	Bear Canyon	36.084°N	121.375°W
Pine Creek	Carmel Valley	36.408°N	121.690°W
Pine Creek	San Ardo	36.066°N	120.936°W
Piney Creek	Sycamore Flat	36.252°N	121.418°W
El Piojo Creek	Burnett Peak	35.830°N	121.148°W
Plaskett Creek	Cape San Martin	35.920°N	121.471°W
Post Creek	Pfeiffer Point	36.243°N	121.774°W
Pozo Hondo Creek	Burnett Peak	35.836°N	121.206°W
Prewitt Creek	Cape San Martin	35.935°N	121.474°W
Puerto Suello Creek	Ventana Cones	36.330°N	121.745°W
Quail Creek	Chualar	36.611°N	121.547°W
Rana Creek	Carmel Valley	36.437°N	121.629°W
Rat Creek	Lopez Point	36.092°N	121.618°W
Rattlesnake Creek	Cone Peak	36.074°N	121.397°W
Rattlesnake Creek	Carmel Valley	36.376°N	121.684°W
Redwood Creek	Partington Ridge	36.247°N	121.674°W
Reliz Creek	Paraiso Springs	36.315°N	121.294°W
Robertson Creek	Rana Creek	36.377°N	121.561°W
Rocky Creek	Soberanes Point	36.380°N	121.901°W
Rocky Creek	Junipero Serra Peak	36.236°N	121.491°W
Roosevelt Creek	Cone Peak	36.124°N	121.469°W
Salinas River	Marina	36.749°N	121.803°W
Salmon Creek	Burro Mountain	35.808°N	121.363°W
Salmon Creek	Burnett Peak	35.848°N	121.193°W
Salsipuedes Creek	Cone Peak	36.060°N	121.434°W
Salsipuedes Creek	Mount Carmel	36.447°N	121.820°W
San Antonio River	Bradley	35.860°N	120.802°W
San Carpoforo Creek	Burro Mountain	35.764°N	121.324°W
San Clemente Creek	Carmel Valley	36.432°N	121.713°W
San Jose Creek	Monterey	36.524°N	121.925°W
San Lorenzo Creek	Thompson Canyon	36.196°N	121.126°W
San Miguel Creek	Alder Peak	35.948°N	121.299°W
Sand Creek	Sycamore Flat	36.263°N	121.430°W
Santa Lucia Creek	Junipero Serra Peak	36.223°N	121.497°W
Santa Lucia Creek	Cone Peak	36.085°N	121.417°W
Sapaque Creek	Bryson	35.796°N	121.094°W
Sargent Creek	Wunpost	35.951°N	120.862°W
Seal Rock Creek	Monterey	36.588°N	121.963°W
Arroyo Seco	Soledad	36.414°N	121.341°W
Seneca Creek	Monterey	36.502°N	121.880°W
Shovel Handle Creek	Zigzag Creek	36.196°N	121.582°W
Sierra Creek	Point Sur	36.365°N	121.886°W
Skinner Creek	Big Sur	36.329°N	121.793°W
Slickrock Creek	Alder Peak	35.979°N	121.350°W
Soberanes Creek	Soberanes Point	36.456°N	121.924°W
Soda Spring Creek	Villa Creek	35.817°N	121.376°W
South Fork Big Sur River	Partington Ridge	36.244°N	121.679°W
South Fork Black Rock Creek	Carmel Valley	36.418°N	121.742°W
South Fork Little Sur River	Big Sur	36.330°N	121.862°W
South Fork Prewitt Creek	Cape San Martin	35.944°N	121.456°W
South Fork Santa Lucia Creek	Junipero Serra Peak	36.200°N	121.474°W
South Fork Waller Creek	Burnett Peak	35.839°N	121.139°W
South Fork Willow Creek	Cape San Martin	35.894°N	121.447°W
Spruce Creek	Villa Creek	35.868°N	121.441°W
Steve Creek	Burnett Peak	35.845°N	121.200°W
Stonewall Creek	Soledad	36.410°N	121.305°W
Stony Creek	Alder Peak	35.928°N	121.276°W
Swamp Creek	Mount Harlan	36.739°N	121.473°W
Sweetwater Creek	Paraiso Springs	36.263°N	121.355°W
Sycamore Creek	Burnett Peak	35.841°N	121.155°W
Tan Oak Creek	Zigzag Creek	36.196°N	121.597°W
Tash Creek	Sycamore Flat	36.301°N	121.474°W
Tassajara Creek	Zigzag Creek	36.219°N	121.501°W
Tembladero Slough	Moss Landing	36.773°N	121.788°W
Terrace Creek	Partington Ridge	36.249°N	121.725°W
Topo Creek	North Chalone Peak	36.388°N	121.163°W
El Toro Creek	Salinas	36.629°N	121.687°W
Tularcitos Creek	Carmel Valley	36.464°N	121.713°W
Turner Creek	Big Sur	36.375°N	121.832°W
Turtle Creek	Bryson	35.799°N	121.107°W
Twin Valley Creek	Burnett Peak	35.870°N	121.173°W
Vaqueros Creek	Paraiso Springs	36.265°N	121.336°W
Ventana Creek	Ventana Cones	36.259°N	121.744°W
Ventana Mesa Creek	Ventana Cones	36.315°N	121.681°W
Vicente Creek	Lopez Point	36.044°N	121.585°W
Villa Creek	Villa Creek	35.849°N	121.408°W
Wagner Creek	Burro Mountain	35.820°N	121.274°W
Waller Creek	Burnett Peak	35.836°N	121.153°W
Waterdog Creek	Bryson	35.795°N	121.104°W
Watson Creek	Spreckels	36.579°N	121.720°W
Watsonville Slough	Moss Landing	36.853°N	121.808°W
Wayland Creek	Smith Mountain	36.017°N	120.590°W

Monterey County Lakes

Water	Location	Latitude	Longitude
Catfish Lake	Parkfield	35.964°N	120.445°W
Covington Lake	Cholame Hills	35.856°N	120.405°W
Crespi Pond	Monterey	36.636°N	121.932°W
Del Monte Lake	Seaside	36.600°N	121.869°W
The Dry Lake	Sycamore Flat	36.274°N	121.424°W
Espinosa Lake	Salinas	36.741°N	121.707°W
El Estero	Monterey	36.599°N	121.884°W
Kenner Lake	Hepsedam Peak	36.266°N	120.846°W
Lagunita Lake	San Juan Bautista	36.775°N	121.601°W
The Lakes	Junipero Serra Peak	36.232°N	121.483°W
Monroe Lake	Priest Valley	36.146°N	120.719°W
Mudhen Lake	Salinas	36.627°N	121.730°W
Laguna Del Rey	Seaside	36.607°N	121.857°W
Roberts Lake	Seaside	36.608°N	121.857°W
El Toro Lake	Spreckels	36.557°N	121.736°W
Warner Lake	Watsonville East	36.880°N	121.742°W

Monterey County Reservoirs

Water	Location	Latitude	Longitude
Coleman Reservoir	Bear Canyon	36.084°N	121.281°W
Forest Lake	Monterey	36.591°N	121.941°W
Lake San Antonio	Tierra Redonda Mtn.	35.799°N	120.885°W
Lower Stoney Creek Res.	Alder Peak	35.958°N	121.276°W
Milpitas Reservoir	Bear Canyon	36.071°N	121.302°W
White Rock Lake	Mount Carmel	36.412°N	121.771°W

San Luis Obispo County Creeks, Streams, Rivers

Water	Location	Latitude	Longitude
Adobe Creek	San Simeon	35.652°N	121.221°W
Alamo Creek	Huasna Peak	35.009°N	120.314°W
Alamo Creek	Santa Margarita Lake	35.327°N	120.441°W
Alva Paul Creek	Morro Bay North	35.398°N	120.866°W
Asbury Creek	Bryson	35.756°N	121.031°W
Atascadero Creek	Templeton	35.505°N	120.660°W
Barrett Creek	Branch Mountain	35.228°N	120.044°W
Beartrap Creek	La Panza	35.335°N	120.140°W
Los Berros Creek	Oceano	35.106°N	120.586°W
Branch Creek	Los Machos Hills	35.145°N	120.180°W
Brizziolari Creek	San Luis Obispo	35.277°N	120.668°W
Broken Bridge Creek	San Simeon	35.642°N	121.182°W
Burnett Creek	San Simeon	35.750°N	121.192°W
Burrito Creek	Lopez Mountain	35.337°N	120.532°W
Caballada Creek	Pebblestone Shut-in	35.745°N	121.094°W
Camatta Creek	Camatta Canyon	35.599°N	120.339°W
Cantinas Creek	Bryson	35.759°N	121.006°W
Carnaza Creek	La Panza Ranch	35.427°N	120.169°W
Carrie Creek	Huasna Peak	35.096°N	120.351°W
Cayucos Creek	Cayucos	35.449°N	120.907°W
Arroyo De Los Chinos	Piedras Blancas	35.725°N	121.316°W
Cholame Creek	Cholame	35.659°N	120.369°W
Chorro Creek	Morro Bay South	35.341°N	120.841°W
Cienega Creek	York Mountain	35.524°N	120.852°W
Coon Creek	Morro Bay South	35.259°N	120.894°W
Corral Creek	Chimney Canyon	35.096°N	120.235°W

Cottontail Creek	Morro Bay North	35.464°N	120.871°W
Dairy Creek	San Luis Obispo	35.325°N	120.733°W
Davenport Creek	Pismo Beach	35.222°N	120.689°W
Arroyo De La Laguna	Piedras Blancas	35.710°N	121.309°W
Deleissigues Creek	Nipomo	35.041°N	120.482°W
Dip Creek	Lime Mountain	35.741°N	120.910°W
Dry Creek	Tar Spring Ridge	35.217°N	120.445°W
Dry Creek	Paso Robles	35.653°N	120.640°W
Eagle Creek	Atascadero	35.438°N	120.694°W
East Branch Huerhuero Creek	Creston	35.518°N	120.520°W
East Corral de Piedra Creek	Arroyo Grande	35.197°N	120.610°W
East Fork Morro Creek	Morro Bay North	35.428°N	120.751°W
Ellysly Creek	Cayucos	35.463°N	120.971°W
Estrella River	Paso Robles	35.742°N	120.691°W
Fernandez Creek	Camatta Ranch	35.458°N	120.333°W
Fish Creek	Chimney Canyon	35.094°N	120.239°W
Franklin Creek	Lime Mountain	35.689°N	120.946°W
Froom Creek	Pismo Beach	35.250°N	120.699°W
Gould Creek	Pebblestone Shut-in	35.748°N	121.078°W
Arroyo Grande Creek	Oceano	35.101°N	120.630°W
Graves Creek	Templeton	35.531°N	120.703°W
Green Valley Creek	Cambria	35.533°N	121.048°W
Hale Creek	Atascadero	35.424°N	120.698°W
Arroyo Hondo	Piedras Blancas	35.750°N	121.314°W
Huasna Creek	Huasna Peak	35.080°N	120.370°W
Huasna River	Huasna Peak	35.016°N	120.328°W
Huerhuero Creek	Paso Robles	35.675°N	120.686°W
Huffs Hole Creek	Tar Spring Ridge	35.214°N	120.456°W
Indian Creek	Shandon	35.645°N	120.479°W
Indian Creek	Shandon	35.654°N	120.450°W
Islay Creek	Morro Bay South	35.276°N	120.888°W
Jack Creek	York Mountain	35.549°N	120.792°W
Jollo Creek	Huasna Peak	35.073°N	120.280°W
Kavanaugh Creek	Pebblestone Shut-in	35.749°N	121.001°W
Kennel Creek	Los Machos Hills	35.183°N	120.177°W
Arroyo Laguna	San Simeon	35.663°N	121.211°W
Las Tablas Creek	Lime Mountain	35.743°N	120.958°W
Leffingwell Creek	Cambria	35.581°N	121.118°W
Little Burnett Creek	Pebblestone Shut-in	35.748°N	121.071°W
Little Cayucos Creek	Cayucos	35.448°N	120.903°W
Little Falls Creek	Tar Spring Ridge	35.246°N	120.487°W
Little Jollo Creek	Chimney Canyon	35.121°N	120.211°W
Little Morro Creek	Morro Bay North	35.379°N	120.851°W
Little Pico Creek	San Simeon	35.634°N	121.163°W
Logan Creek	Los Machos Hills	35.140°N	120.154°W
Los Machos Creek	Los Machos Hills	35.184°N	120.154°W
Mariana Creek	Pozo Summit	35.358°N	120.275°W
Marmolejo Creek	San Simeon	35.699°N	121.171°W
McGinnis Creek	Camatta Ranch	35.381°N	120.280°W
Meadow Creek	Oceano	35.112°N	120.625°W
Mehlschau Creek	Nipomo	35.057°N	120.500°W
Middle Branch Huerhuero Creek	Creston	35.518°N	120.520°W
Moreno Creek	Santa Margarita	35.410°N	120.568°W
Morro Creek	Morro Bay North	35.376°N	120.863°W
Mustard Creek	Paso Robles	35.665°N	120.695°W
Navajo Creek	La Panza Ranch	35.500°N	120.198°W
New River	New Cuyama	34.973°N	119.671°W
Nipomo Creek	Santa Maria	34.994°N	120.439°W
North Fork Pico Creek	Pico Creek	35.624°N	121.136°W
No. Fk. San Simeon Crk.	Pebblestone Shut-in	35.627°N	121.052°W
North Grizzly Bend Creek	Bryson	35.750°N	121.052°W
Oak Knoll Creek	San Simeon	35.651°N	121.219°W
Old Creek	Cayucos	35.435°N	120.886°W
Oso Creek	Caldwell Mesa	35.174°N	120.279°W
Oso Flaco Creek	Oceano	35.032°N	120.633°W
Arroyo Del Oso	Piedras Blancas	35.691°N	121.289°W
Los Osos Creek	Morro Bay South	35.338°N	120.827°W
Arroyo Del Padre Juan	Pico Creek	35.612°N	121.145°W
Paloma Creek	Atascadero	35.468°N	120.629°W
Paso Robles Creek	Templeton	35.532°N	120.705°W
Pecho Creek	Port San Luis	35.179°N	120.792°W
Pennington Creek	Morro Bay South	35.325°N	120.752°W
Perry Creek	Cambria	35.565°N	121.074°W

Phoenix Creek	Tar Spring Ridge	35.184°N	120.444°W
Pico Creek	Pico Creek	35.616°N	121.148°W
Pilitas Creek	Lopez Mountain	35.350°N	120.511°W
Pine Creek	Estrella	35.654°N	120.508°W
Pine Creek	Caldwell Mesa	35.166°N	120.320°W
Pismo Creek	Pismo Beach	35.134°N	120.640°W
Placer Creek	La Panza	35.352°N	120.141°W
Potrero Creek	Lopez Mountain	35.286°N	120.543°W
Potrero Creek	Tar Spring Ridge	35.189°N	120.433°W
Pozo Creek	Santa Margarita Lake	35.295°N	120.389°W
Prefumo Creek	Pismo Beach	35.244°N	120.680°W
Arryo del Puerto	San Simeon	35.643°N	121.188°W
Quail Water Creek	Shedd Canyon	35.522°N	120.399°W
Rafael Creek	California Valley	35.251°N	120.072°W
Rinconada Creek	Lopez Mountain	35.361°N	120.533°W
Rioly Run	Cambria	35.617°N	121.066°W
Rogers Creek	California Valley	35.276°N	120.089°W
Salsipuedes Creek	Santa Margarita Lake	35.315°N	120.466°W
Salt Creek	Caldwell Mesa	35.230°N	120.347°W
San Bernardo Creek	Morro Bay South	35.357°N	120.811°W
San Jacinto Creek	Paso Robles	35.728°N	120.657°W
San Juan Creek	Cholame	35.659°N	120.369°W
San Luis Obispo Creek	Pismo Beach	35.179°N	120.737°W
San Luisito Creek	Morro Bay South	35.354°N	120.793°W
San Marcos Creek	Paso Robles	35.721°N	120.694°W
San Simeon Creek	Pico Creek	35.595°N	121.126°W
Sand Creek	Packwood Creek	35.500°N	120.096°W
Santa Margarita Creek	Santa Margarita	35.444°N	120.605°W
Santa Rita Creek	York Mountain	35.537°N	120.752°W
Santa Rosa Creek	Cambria	35.569°N	121.110°W
Saucelito Creek	Tar Spring Ridge	35.204°N	120.425°W
Arroyo Seco	Caldwell Mesa	35.141°N	120.359°W
Sheep Creek	Los Machos Hills	35.185°N	120.178°W
Sheepcamp Creek	York Mountain	35.551°N	120.775°W
Shell Creek	Camatta Ranch	35.486°N	120.326°W
Smith Creek	Morro Bay North	35.442°N	120.831°W
Snake Creek	Lime Mountain	35.740°N	120.907°W
South Fork Pico Creek	Pico Creek	35.624°N	121.136°W
South Fork San Simeon Creek	Pebblestone	35.625°N	121.023°W
South Fork Santa Rita Creek	York Mountain	35.500°N	120.788°W
Spanish Cabin Creek	San Simeon	35.716°N	121.162°W
Steiner Creek	Cambria	35.609°N	121.072°W
Stenner Creek	San Luis Obispo	35.303°N	120.666°W
Stony Creek	Caldwell Mesa	35.201°N	120.349°W
Suey Creek	Santa Maria	34.971°N	120.399°W
Summit Creek	York Mountain	35.578°N	120.833°W
Sycamore Creek	Miranda Pine Mtn.	35.089°N	120.039°W
Tar Spring Creek	Arroyo Grande NE	35.134°N	120.550°W
Tassajera Creek	Atascadero	35.377°N	120.645°W
Temettate Creek	Nipomo	35.077°N	120.430°W
Tobacco Creek	Pebblestone Shut-in	35.743°N	121.096°W
Toro Creek	Santa Margarita Lake	35.322°N	120.424°W
Toro Creek	Morro Bay North	35.413°N	120.873°W
Town Creek	Lime Mountain	35.719°N	120.956°W
Trout Creek	Santa Margarita	35.441°N	120.607°W
Trout Creek	Caldwell Mesa	35.201°N	120.349°W
Trujillo Creek	Pozo Summit	35.313°N	120.348°W
Van Gordon Creek	Cambria	35.594°N	121.119°W
Vasquez Creek	Tar Spring Ridge	35.208°N	120.483°W
Villa Creek	Cayucos	35.460°N	120.969°W
Villa Creek	Arroyo Grande NE	35.234°N	120.556°W
Walnut Creek	La Panza NE	35.459°N	120.012°W
The Wash	Cuyama	34.954°N	119.604°W
West Branch Huerhuero Creek	Creston	35.549°N	120.537°W
West Corral de Piedra Creek	Arroyo Grande NE	35.197°N	120.610°W
West Fork Burnett Creek	San Simeon	35.740°N	121.196°W
Wild Hog Creek	Branch Mountain	35.221°N	120.044°W
Willow Creek	Cayucos	35.428°N	120.882°W
Willow Creek	York Mountain	35.551°N	120.773°W
Windmill Creek	La Panza Ranch	35.427°N	120.224°W
Wittenberg Creek	Tar Spring Ridge	35.214°N	120.457°W
Yaro Creek	Santa Margarita Lake	35.343°N	120.398°W
Yeguas Creek	La Panza NE	35.459°N	120.012°W

San Luis Obispo County Lakes

Water	Location	Latitude	Longitude
Beck Lake	Santa Margarita	35.491°N	120.534°W
Big Pocket Lake	Oceano	35.083°N	120.614°W
Big Twin Lake	Oceano	35.070°N	120.608°W
Black Lake	Oceano	35.058°N	120.603°W
Bolsa Chica Lake	Oceano	35.067°N	120.603°W
Celery Lake	Oceano	35.071°N	120.602°W
Clear Lake	Santa Margarita	35.476°N	120.521°W
Dune Lakes	Oceano	35.068°N	120.608°W
Grant Lake (historical)	Holland Canyon	35.598°N	120.152°W
Hospital Lake	Oceano	35.071°N	120.612°W
Jack Lake	Oceano	35.039°N	120.603°W
Kerr Lake	Cholame Valley	35.776°N	120.359°W
Lettuce Lake	Oceano	35.036°N	120.608°W
Little Oso Flaco Lake	Oceano	35.031°N	120.609°W
Long Lake	Orchard Peak	35.680°N	120.232°W
Mud Lake	Oceano	35.063°N	120.611°W
O'Brien Lake	Orchard Peak	35.673°N	120.227°W
Oso Flaco Lake	Oceano	35.029°N	120.621°W
Pipeline Lake	Oceano	35.074°N	120.606°W
Poison Water Pond	Orchard Peak	35.741°N	120.234°W
Poso Ortega	Packwood Creek	35.521°N	120.094°W
Silver Lake	Santa Margarita	35.481°N	120.522°W
Small Twin Lake	Oceano	35.069°N	120.604°W
Soda Lake	Chimineas Ranch	35.235°N	119.892°W
Twisselmann Lake	Orchard Peak	35.662°N	120.213°W
White Lake	Oceano	35.066°N	120.608°W
Willow Lake	Oceano	35.079°N	120.614°W

San Luis Obispo County Reservoirs

Water	Location	Latitude	Longitude
Atascadero Lake	Atascadero	35.468°N	120.667°W
Chorro Reservoir	San Luis Obispo	35.336°N	120.686°W
Eto Lake	Morro Bay South	35.318°N	120.812°W
Laguna Lake	San Luis Obispo	35.260°N	120.683°W
Nacimiento Lake	Tierra Redonda Mtn.	35.759°N	120.884°W
Lake Ysabel (historical)	Templeton	35.589°N	120.676°W
Lopez Lake	Tar Spring Ridge	35.187°N	120.486°W
Lopez Reservoir	Arroyo Grande NE	35.170°N	120.533°W
Quail Spring Reservoir	Cuyama	34.991°N	119.553°W
Santa Margarita Lake	Lopez Mountain	35.338°N	120.501°W
Twitchell Reservoir	Dixie Mountain	39.987°N	120.322°W
Whale Rock Reservoir	Cayucos	35.448°N	120.884°W

Santa Barbara County Creeks, Streams, Rivers

Water	Location	Latitude	Longitude
Abadi Creek	Old Man Mountain	34.609°N	119.384°W
Alamo Creek	Santa Rosa Hills	34.519°N	120.306°W
Alamo Pintado Creek	Solvang	34.585°N	120.134°W
Alder Creek	Carpinteria	34.487°N	119.524°W
Alisal Creek	Solvang	34.585°N	120.143°W
Aliso Creek	Chimney Canyon	35.032°N	120.187°W
Los Amoles Creek	Santa Rosa Hills	34.562°N	120.364°W
Asphaltum Creek	Foxen Canyon	34.856°N	120.240°W
Atascadero Creek	Goleta	34.420°N	119.828°W
Atascoso Creek	Santa Rosa Hills	34.518°N	120.313°W
Ballard Creek	Los Olivos	34.750°N	120.018°W
Ballinger Canyon Wash	Cuyama	34.879°N	119.507°W
Bear Creek	San Marcos Pass	34.544°N	119.859°W
Bear Creek	Surf	34.648°N	120.601°W
Bear Creek	Madulce Peak	34.713°N	119.515°W
Bitter Creek	New Cuyama	34.971°N	119.716°W
Branch Canyon Wash	New Cuyama	34.971°N	119.711°W
La Brea Creek	Foxen Canyon	34.850°N	120.200°W
Buckhorn Creek	Little Pine Mountain	34.578°N	119.669°W
Arroyo El Bulito	Sacate	34.463°N	120.332°W
Arroyo Burro	Santa Barbara	34.428°N	119.750°W
Cachuma Creek	Lake Cachuma	34.606°N	119.936°W
Calabazal Creek	Santa Ynez	34.589°N	120.039°W
El Callejon Creek	Santa Rosa Hills	34.532°N	120.285°W
Camuesa Creek	Little Pine Mountain	34.528°N	119.664°W
El Capitan Creek	Tajiguas	34.458°N	120.021°W
Carneros Creek	Santa Paula Peak	34.417°N	119.087°W
Carpinteria Creek	Carpinteria	34.390°N	119.519°W
Cieneguitas Creek	Goleta	34.434°N	119.774°W
Clear Creek	Miranda Pine Mnt.	35.097°N	120.124°W
Coche Creek	San Rafael Mountain	34.664°N	119.764°W
Cold Springs Creek	Santa Barbara	34.459°N	119.653°W
Cuaslui Creek	Zaca Creek	34.749°N	120.204°W
Cuyama River	Twitchell Dam	34.903°N	120.311°W
Davy Brown Creek	Bald Mountain	34.772°N	119.943°W
Dry Creek	Goleta	34.467°N	119.857°W
Dry Creek	Zaca Creek	34.637°N	120.184°W
Dry Creek	Zaca Lake	34.803°N	120.004°W
East Fork Fish Creek	Bald Mountain	34.754°N	119.909°W
East Fork Maria Ygnacio Creek	Goleta	34.459°N	119.793°W
East Fork Santa Cruz Creek	Big Pine Mountain	34.641°N	119.750°W
Eldorado Creek	White Ledge Peak	34.424°N	119.474°W
Escondido Creek	Lompoc Hills	34.514°N	120.454°W
Espada Creek	Lompoc Hills	34.512°N	120.490°W
Figueroa Creek	Los Olivos	34.686°N	120.035°W
Fish Creek	Bald Mountain	34.760°N	119.902°W
Franklin Creek	Carpinteria	34.396°N	119.528°W
Garrapata Creek	Carpinteria	34.433°N	119.571°W
Gasper Creek	Lompoc Hills	34.513°N	120.474°W
Gaviotito Creek	Santa Rosa Hills	34.516°N	120.315°W
Gidney Creek	Little Pine Mountain	34.526°N	119.673°W
Gobernador Creek	White Ledge Peak	34.401°N	119.485°W
Grapevine Creek	Big Pine Mountain	34.659°N	119.718°W
Canada Honda Creek	Point Arguello	34.609°N	120.637°W
Hot Springs Creek	Solvang	34.506°N	120.222°W
Hot Springs Creek	Santa Barbara	34.443°N	119.649°W
La Hoya Creek	Lompoc Hills	34.581°N	120.408°W
Indian Creek	Little Pine Mountain	34.534°N	119.632°W
Jalama Creek	Tranquillon Mountain	34.511°N	120.502°W
El Jaro Creek	Lompoc Hills	34.584°N	120.407°W
Kelly Creek	San Marcos Pass	34.542°N	119.854°W
Lacosca Creek	Madulce Peak	34.630°N	119.510°W
Las Canovas Creek	Solvang	34.505°N	120.226°W
Las Vegas Creek	Goleta	34.436°N	119.831°W
Lisque Creek	Los Olivos	34.688°N	120.036°W
Llanito Creek	Santa Rosa Hills	34.532°N	120.285°W
Manzana Creek	Bald Mountain	34.828°N	119.994°W
Maria Ygnacio Creek	Goleta	34.425°N	119.809°W
Mission Creek	Santa Barbara	34.413°N	119.687°W
Monjas Creek	Solvang	34.543°N	120.136°W
Mono Creek	Little Pine Mountain	34.520°N	119.632°W
Montecito Creek	Santa Barbara	34.417°N	119.633°W
Morse Creek	Carpinteria	34.485°N	119.514°W
Nojoqui Creek	Solvang	34.606°N	120.192°W
North Fork Juncal Creek	Carpinteria	34.494°N	119.501°W
North Fork La Brea Creek	Tepusquet Canyon	34.881°N	120.131°W
Oak Creek	Santa Barbara	34.419°N	119.626°W
Orcutt Creek	Guadalupe	34.903°N	120.523°W
Palos Colorados Creek	Santa Rosa Hills	34.573°N	120.369°W
Arroyo Paredon	Carpinteria	34.413°N	119.556°W
Picay Creek	Carpinteria	34.434°N	119.596°W
Quiota Creek	Santa Ynez	34.581°N	120.109°W
Romero Creek	Carpinteria	34.419°N	119.620°W
Salisbury Canyon Wash	New Cuyama	34.952°N	119.694°W
Salsipuedes Creek	Lompoc	34.632°N	120.412°W
San Antonio Creek	Goleta	34.441°N	119.804°W
San Antonio Creek	Casmalia	34.802°N	120.618°W
San Jose Creek	Goleta	34.424°N	119.828°W
San Lucas Creek	Santa Ynez	34.592°N	120.015°W
San Miguelito Creek	Lompoc	34.664°N	120.480°W
San Pedro Creek	Goleta	34.417°N	119.824°W
San Roque Creek	Santa Barbara	34.438°N	119.746°W
San Ysidro Creek	Carpinteria	34.419°N	119.624°W
Santa Agueda Creek	Santa Ynez	34.588°N	120.032°W
Santa Cruz Creek	Lake Cachuma	34.589°N	119.915°W
Santa Maria River	Point Sal	34.971°N	120.649°W
Santa Monica Creek	Carpinteria	34.396°N	119.536°W

Water	Location	Latitude	Longitude
Santa Rosa Creek	Santa Rosa Hills	34.609°N	120.286°W
Canada De Santa Rosa	Los Alamos	34.743°N	120.306°W
Santa Ynez River	Surf	34.692°N	120.601°W
Sheep Camp Creek	Miranda Pine Mtn.	35.034°N	120.121°W
Sisquoc River	Twitchell Dam	34.903°N	120.311°W
South Fork La Brea Creek	Tepusquet Canyon	34.881°N	120.131°W
South Fork Sisquoc River	Hurricane Deck	34.760°N	119.772°W
Steer Creek	White Ledge Peak	34.424°N	119.474°W
Sulphur Creek	Zaca Lake	34.801°N	120.008°W
Sutton Creek	White Ledge Peak	34.429°N	119.491°W
Sweetwater Creek	Lake Cachuma	34.580°N	119.972°W
Sycamore Creek	Santa Barbara	34.417°N	119.666°W
Tajiguas Creek	Tajiguas	34.464°N	120.100°W
Tecolotito Creek	Goleta	34.427°N	119.849°W
Tepusquet Creek	Sisquoc	34.862°N	120.255°W
Toro Canyon Creek	Carpinteria	34.415°N	119.566°W
Wells Creek	Peak Mountain	34.962°N	119.775°W
West Fork Mill Creek	Bald Mountain	34.801°N	119.999°W
West Fork Santa Cruz Creek	San Rafael Mtn.	34.642°N	119.750°W
Yridisis Creek	Santa Rosa Hills	34.525°N	120.297°W
Ytias Creek	Santa Rosa Hills	34.547°N	120.357°W
Zaca Creek	Solvang	34.608°N	120.205°W
Zanja de Cota Creek	Santa Ynez	34.586°N	120.102°W

Santa Barbara County Lakes

Water	Location	Latitude	Longitude
Laguna Blanca	Goleta	34.431°N	119.759°W
Devereux Lagoon	Dos Pueblos Canyon	34.414°N	119.875°W
Guadalupe Lake	Guadalupe	34.912°N	120.536°W
Zaca Lake	Zaca Lake	34.778°N	120.039°W

Santa Barbara County Reservoirs

Water	Location	Latitude	Longitude
Buell Reservoir	Carpinteria	34.444°N	119.569°W
Carpinteria Reservoir	White Ledge Peak	34.407°N	119.485°W
Dennis Reservoir	Goleta	34.475°N	119.820°W
Gibraltar Reservoir	Little Pine Mountain	34.527°N	119.686°W
Glen Anne Reservoir	Dos Pueblos Canyon	34.472°N	119.913°W
Glen Annie Reservoir	Dos Pueblos Canyon	34.471°N	119.879°W
Jameson Lake	Carpinteria	34.489°N	119.505°W
Jameson Lake	Carpinteria	34.483°N	119.507°W
Lake Cachuma	Lake Cachuma	34.587°N	119.980°W
Lake Los Carneros	Goleta	34.442°N	119.848°W
Lauro Canyon Reservoir	Santa Barbara	34.454°N	119.726°W
Lauro Reservoir	Goleta	34.467°N	119.777°W
Ortega Reservoir	Carpinteria	34.432°N	119.592°W
Park Lane Reservoir	Carpinteria	34.448°N	119.616°W
Romero Reservoir	Carpinteria	34.447°N	119.597°W
Sheffield Reservoir	Santa Barbara	34.445°N	119.690°W
Vic Trace Reservoir	Santa Barbara	34.405°N	119.714°W

Santa Cruz County Creeks, Streams, Rivers

Water	Location	Latitude	Longitude
Agua Puera Creek	Davenport	37.023°N	122.214°W
Alba Creek	Felton	37.103°N	122.103°W
Amaya Creek	Laurel	37.075°N	121.924°W
Aptos Creek	Soquel	36.970°N	121.905°W
Archibald Creek	Davenport	37.054°N	122.225°W
Baldwin Creek	Santa Cruz	36.966°N	122.122°W
Bates Creek	Soquel	36.996°N	121.953°W
Bean Creek	Felton	37.051°N	122.060°W
Bear Creek	Castle Rock Ridge	37.128°N	122.121°W
Bennett Creek	Felton	37.051°N	122.084°W
Berry Creek	Davenport	37.077°N	122.219°W
Berry Creek	Franklin Point	37.168°N	122.263°W
Big Creek	Davenport	37.067°N	122.229°W
Blooms Creek	Big Basin	37.165°N	122.224°W
Borregas Creek	Soquel	36.978°N	121.927°W
Boulder Brook	Felton	37.037°N	122.071°W
Boulder Creek	Castle Rock Ridge	37.127°N	122.120°W
Boyer Creek	Davenport	37.094°N	122.206°W
Bracken Brae Creek	Big Basin	37.139°N	122.144°W
Branciforte Creek	Santa Cruz	36.987°N	122.013°W
Bridge Creek	Laurel	37.030°N	121.900°W
Browns Creek	Watsonville West	36.995°N	121.801°W
Bull Creek	Felton	37.053°N	122.071°W
Burns Creek	Laurel	37.119°N	121.960°W
Carbonera Creek	Santa Cruz	36.974°N	122.021°W
Casserly Creek	Watsonville East	36.954°N	121.743°W
Clear Creek	Felton	37.110°N	122.107°W
Corralitos Creek	Watsonville East	36.935°N	121.742°W
Coward Creek	Watsonville East	36.914°N	121.711°W
Crystal Creek	Laurel	37.028°N	121.987°W
Deans Creek	Felton	37.092°N	122.101°W
Deer Creek	Castle Rock Ridge	37.171°N	122.074°W
Eagle Creek	Felton	37.031°N	122.055°W
East Branch Liddell Creek	Davenport	37.009°N	122.163°W
East Waddell Creek	Franklin Point	37.134°N	122.267°W
Fall Creek	Felton	37.059°N	122.077°W
Ferndell Creek	Felton	37.051°N	122.061°W
Foreman Creek	Big Basin	37.130°N	122.133°W
Fritch Creek	Felton	37.111°N	122.089°W
Gaffey Creek	Watsonville East	36.990°N	121.735°W
Gallighan Slough	Watsonville West	36.906°N	121.804°W
Gold Gulch Creek	Felton	37.040°N	122.068°W
Granite Creek	Laurel	37.018°N	121.996°W
Hanson Slough	Watsonville West	36.897°N	121.791°W
Hare Creek	Big Basin	37.153°N	122.161°W
Harkins Slough	Watsonville West	36.890°N	121.801°W
Henry Creek	Franklin Point	37.161°N	122.272°W
Hester Creek	Laurel	37.055°N	121.939°W
Hinckley Creek	Laurel	37.055°N	121.921°W
Hughes Creek	Watsonville East	36.965°N	121.747°W
Jamison Creek	Big Basin	37.146°N	122.156°W
Kelly Creek	Big Basin	37.172°N	122.250°W
Kings Creek	Big Basin	37.155°N	122.133°W
Laguna Creek	Santa Cruz	36.983°N	122.153°W
Last Chance Creek	Franklin Point	37.138°N	122.258°W
Laurel Creek	Laurel	37.119°N	121.960°W
Liddell Creek	Davenport	37.000°N	122.181°W
Little Creek	Davenport	37.063°N	122.228°W
Logan Creek	Castle Rock Ridge	37.184°N	122.123°W
Lompico Creek	Felton	37.082°N	122.050°W
Love Creek	Felton	37.088°N	122.086°W
Mackenzie Creek	Felton	37.072°N	122.016°W
Maddocks Creek	Big Basin	37.185°N	122.218°W
Majors Creek	Santa Cruz	36.977°N	122.140°W
Malosky Creek	Felton	37.115°N	122.116°W
Manson Creek	Felton	37.070°N	122.084°W
Marshall Creek	Felton	37.091°N	122.092°W
Meder Creek	Santa Cruz	36.962°N	122.082°W
Mill Creek	Davenport	37.077°N	122.243°W
Mill Creek	Davenport	37.042°N	122.173°W
Mill Creek	Felton	37.111°N	122.047°W
Molino Creek	Davenport	37.037°N	122.227°W
Moore Creek	Santa Cruz	36.950°N	122.058°W
Newell Creek	Felton	37.081°N	122.079°W
Opal Creek	Big Basin	37.165°N	122.224°W
Pajaro River	Moss Landing	36.850°N	121.809°W
Peavine Creek	Big Basin	37.138°N	122.142°W
Peters Creek	Mindego Hill	37.251°N	122.217°W
Powder Mill Creek	Felton	37.008°N	122.042°W
Quail Hollow Creek	Felton	37.077°N	122.053°W
Reggiardo Creek	Davenport	37.023°N	122.131°W
Rider Creek	Loma Prieta	37.016°N	121.816°W
Rogers Creek	Big Basin	37.193°N	122.218°W
Ruins Creek	Felton	37.057°N	122.030°W
Salsipuedes Creek	Watsonville East	36.910°N	121.744°W
San Lorenzo River	Santa Cruz	36.964°N	122.011°W
San Vicente Creek	Davenport	37.009°N	122.193°W
Scott Creek	Davenport	37.042°N	122.226°W
Sempervirens Creek	Big Basin	37.168°N	122.212°W
Shear Creek	Castle Rock Ridge	37.184°N	122.055°W

Shingle Mill Creek	Felton	37.044°N	122.071°W
Silver Creek	Big Basin	37.134°N	122.139°W
Smith Creek	Felton	37.099°N	122.085°W
Soquel Creek	Soquel	36.972°N	121.951°W
Spring Creek	Big Basin	37.148°N	122.136°W
Stapling Creek	Castle Rock Ridge	37.194°N	122.124°W
Struve Slough	Watsonville West	36.900°N	121.783°W
Timms Creek	Franklin Point	37.178°N	122.251°W
Trout Creek	Soquel	36.976°N	121.896°W
Two Bar Creek	Big Basin	37.142°N	122.131°W
Union Creek	Big Basin	37.175°N	122.208°W
Valencia Creek	Soquel	36.977°N	121.896°W
Waterman Creek	Big Basin	37.214°N	122.175°W
West Branch Struve Slough	Watsonville West	36.906°N	121.782°W
West Liddell Creek	Davenport	37.003°N	122.176°W
West Waddell Creek	Franklin Point	37.134°N	122.266°W
Wilder Creek	Santa Cruz	36.953°N	122.075°W
Winter Creek	Davenport	37.058°N	122.226°W
Yellow Bank Creek	Santa Cruz	36.994°N	122.167°W
Zayante Creek	Felton	37.048°N	122.067°W

Santa Cruz County Lakes

Water	Location	Latitude	Longitude
Bonita Lagoon	Soquel	36.961°N	121.991°W
Brush Lagoon (historical)	Laurel	37.080°N	121.931°W
Buzzard Lagoon	Loma Prieta	37.046°N	121.833°W
College Lake	Watsonville East	36.947°N	121.747°W
Corcoran Lagoon	Soquel	36.962°N	121.981°W
Corralitos Lagoon	Watsonville West	36.966°N	121.813°W
Drew Lake	Watsonville East	36.937°N	121.731°W
Kelly Lake	Watsonville East	36.939°N	121.734°W
Laguna del Sargento	Los Gatos	37.137°N	121.986°W
Moran Lake	Soquel	36.957°N	121.975°W
Schwan Lagoon	Soquel	36.965°N	121.994°W
Simas Lake	Watsonville East	36.998°N	121.738°W
Soda Lake	Chittenden	36.908°N	121.607°W
Laguna de las Trancas	Point Ano Nuevo	37.088°N	122.258°W
Lake Tynan	Watsonville East	36.929°N	121.727°W
Whites Lagoon	Laurel	37.047°N	121.878°W
Woods Lagoon	Santa Cruz	36.967°N	122.001°W
Younger Lagoon	Santa Cruz	36.951°N	122.066°W

Santa Cruz County Reservoirs

Water	Location	Latitude	Longitude
Antonelli Pond	Santa Cruz	36.955°N	122.059°W
Bay Street Reservoir	Santa Cruz	36.976°N	122.048°W
Lake Lompico	Felton	37.103°N	122.046°W
Loch Lomond	Felton	37.103°N	122.072°W
Millpond Lake	Laurel	37.052°N	121.925°W
Pinto Lake	Watsonville West	36.951°N	121.767°W
Rose Reservoir	Watsonville East	36.967°N	121.739°W
Sempervirens Reservoir	Big Basin	37.190°N	122.207°W
Spring Lakes	Felton	37.046°N	122.032°W

Ventura County Creeks, Streams, Rivers

Water	Location	Latitude	Longitude
Adobe Creek	Wheeler Springs	34.606°N	119.364°W
Agua Blanca Creek	Cobblestone Mountain	34.541°N	118.761°W
Alamo Creek	Lockwood Valley	34.673°N	119.016°W
Alamo Creek	Reyes Peak	34.690°N	119.292°W
Alder Creek	Devils Heart Peak	34.565°N	118.954°W
Amargosa Creek	Lockwood Valley	34.734°N	119.078°W
Ayers Creek	Ventura	34.372°N	119.346°W
Bear Creek	Fillmore	34.482°N	118.889°W
Bear Creek	Wheeler Springs	34.513°N	119.273°W
Bear Creek	Wheeler Springs	34.513°N	119.272°W
Beardsley Wash	Camarillo	34.209°N	119.114°W
Beartrap Creek	Reyes Peak	34.690°N	119.292°W
Big Cedar Creek	Alamo Mountain	34.657°N	118.907°W

Boulder Creek	Fillmore	34.384°N	118.953°W
Buck Creek	Black Mountain	34.665°N	118.823°W
Burro Creek	Wheeler Springs	34.593°N	119.313°W
Calleguas Creek	Point Mugu	34.098°N	119.087°W
Cannon Creek	Wheeler Springs	34.518°N	119.271°W
Casitas Creek	White Ledge Peak	34.396°N	119.454°W
Catharina Creek	White Ledge Peak	34.430°N	119.444°W
Cedar Creek	Lockwood Valley	34.638°N	119.101°W
Centennial Creek	Fillmore	34.461°N	118.910°W
Cherry Creek	Wheeler Springs	34.605°N	119.356°W
Chismahoo Creek	Matilija	34.384°N	119.355°W
Coldwater Fork	Devils Heart Peak	34.583°N	118.991°W
Conejo Creek	Camarillo	34.190°N	119.021°W
Arroyo Conejo	Newbury Park	34.229°N	118.938°W
Coyote Creek	Ventura	34.354°N	119.310°W
Dead Horse Creek	Alamo Mountain	34.675°N	118.875°W
Derrydale Creek	Wheeler Springs	34.584°N	119.262°W
Dry Creek	Black Mountain	34.701°N	118.870°W
East Fork Alder Creek	Devils Heart Peak	34.577°N	118.939°W
East Fork Coyote Creek	Matilija	34.421°N	119.375°W
Elm Creek	Fillmore	34.493°N	118.885°W
Fish Creek	Cobblestone Mountain	34.609°N	118.796°W
Fourfork Creek	Fillmore	34.461°N	118.910°W
Frazier Creek	Alamo Mountain	34.689°N	118.912°W
Howard Creek	Lion Canyon	34.555°N	119.205°W
Lacosca Creek	Cobblestone Mountain	34.548°N	118.816°W
Ladybug Creek	Wheeler Springs	34.596°N	119.330°W
Laguna Creek	White Ledge Peak	34.407°N	119.445°W
Lake Eleanor Creek	Thousand Oaks	34.146°N	118.849°W
Lion Creek	Ojai	34.435°N	119.196°W
Little Mutau Creek	Lockwood Valley	34.656°N	119.025°W
Little Sespe Creek	Fillmore	34.452°N	118.924°W
Lockwood Creek	Alamo Mountain	34.699°N	118.997°W
Maple Creek	Fillmore	34.492°N	118.916°W
Matilija Creek	Matilija	34.485°N	119.299°W
Michael Creek	Cobblestone Mountain	34.547°N	118.770°W
Middle Fork Lockwood Creek	Lockwood Valley	34.734°N	119.096°W
Munson Creek	Wheeler Springs	34.589°N	119.291°W
Mutau Creek	Lockwood Valley	34.682°N	119.019°W
Negro Creek	Lockwood Valley	34.667°N	119.042°W
North Fork Arroyo Conejo	Newbury Park	34.213°N	118.926°W
North Fork Fish Creek	Cobblestone Mountain	34.609°N	118.809°W
North Fork Lockwood Creek	Lockwood Valley	34.731°N	119.092°W
North Fork Matilija Creek	Matilija	34.485°N	119.298°W
North Fork Piedra Blanca Creek	Lion Canyon	34.588°N	119.162°W
North Fork Santa Ana Creek	Matilija	34.454°N	119.346°W
North Fork Tar Creek	Cobblestone Mountain	34.521°N	118.868°W
North Fork Tar Creek	Fillmore	34.495°N	118.894°W
Oak Creek	Rancho Nuevo Creek	34.727°N	119.390°W
Park Creek	Topatopa Mountains	34.570°N	119.024°W
Piedra Blanca Creek	Lion Canyon	34.559°N	119.152°W
Piru Creek	Piru	34.399°N	118.785°W
Pole Creek	Fillmore	34.392°N	118.902°W
Poplar Creek	Devils Heart Peak	34.595°N	118.999°W
Poplin Creek	Matilija	34.413°N	119.359°W
Arroyo Las Posas	Camarillo	34.239°N	119.006°W
Potrero John Creek	Wheeler Springs	34.585°N	119.268°W
Rancho Nuevo Creek	Rancho Nuevo Creek	34.705°N	119.383°W
Real Wash	Piru	34.397°N	118.801°W
Redrock Creek	Devils Heart Peak	34.500°N	118.900°W
Reeves Creek	Ojai	34.448°N	119.194°W
Revolon Slough	Camarillo	34.128°N	119.077°W
Reyes Creek	Reyes Peak	34.697°N	119.325°W
Rincon Creek	Pitas Point	34.373°N	119.476°W
Rock Creek	Lion Canyon	34.555°N	119.203°W
Rock Creek	Lockwood Valley	34.674°N	119.043°W
Rose Creek	Alamo Mountain	34.674°N	118.880°W
Rose Valley Creek	Lion Canyon	34.551°N	119.208°W
San Antonio Creek	Matilija	34.380°N	119.307°W
San Guillermo Creek	Lockwood Valley	34.732°N	119.088°W
Santa Ana Creek	Matilija	34.408°N	119.339°W

Santa Clara River	Oxnard OE W	34.235°N	119.263°W
Santa Paula Creek	Santa Paula	34.349°N	119.049°W
Arroyo Santa Rosa	Newbury Park	34.233°N	118.925°W
Los Sauces Creek	Pitas Point	34.348°N	119.421°W
Sespe Creek	Fillmore	34.381°N	118.953°W
Seymour Creek	Lockwood Valley	34.734°N	119.040°W
Sheep Creek	Lockwood Valley	34.673°N	119.036°W
Arroyo Simi	Moorpark	34.269°N	118.914°W
Sisar Creek	Ojai	34.428°N	119.090°W
Smith Fork	Black Mountain	34.702°N	118.866°W
Snowy Creek	Black Mountain	34.694°N	118.861°W
South Branch Arroyo Conejo	Newbury Park	34.189°N	118.906°W
Spring Canyon Creek	Fillmore	34.495°N	118.894°W
Squaw Creek	Devils Heart Peak	34.528°N	118.907°W
Stone Corral Creek	Devils Heart Peak	34.558°N	118.943°W
Sulphur Creek	White Ledge Peak	34.409°N	119.445°W
Sulphur Creek	Cobblestone Mountain	34.551°N	118.824°W
Sycamore Creek	Topatopa Mountains	34.567°N	119.051°W
Sycamore Creek	Ojai	34.436°N	119.162°W
Tar Creek	Fillmore	34.491°N	118.941°W
Thacher Creek	Ojai	34.443°N	119.230°W
Timber Creek	Topatopa Mountains	34.557°N	119.069°W
Tinta Creek	Rancho Nuevo Creek	34.704°N	119.389°W
Trout Creek	Lion Canyon	34.559°N	119.143°W
Tule Creek	Wheeler Springs	34.559°N	119.267°W
Upper North Fork Matilija Creek	Old Man Mountain	34.509°N	119.383°W
Ventura River	Ventura	34.276°N	119.307°W
West Fork Arroyo Sequit	Triunfo Pass	34.084°N	118.917°W
West Fork Coyote Creek	White Ledge Peak	34.421°N	119.381°W
West Fork Matilija Creek	Old Man Mountain	34.506°N	119.382°W
West Fork Santa Ana Creek	Matilija	34.454°N	119.346°W
West Fork Sespe Creek	Devils Heart Peak	34.505°N	118.964°W
Willow Creek	Matilija	34.388°N	119.356°W
Willow Creek	Old Man Mountain	34.617°N	119.396°W

Ventura County Lakes

Water	Location	Latitude	Longitude
Lower Rose Lake	Lion Canyon	34.543°N	119.186°W
Matilija Lake	Matilija	34.484°N	119.308°W
McGrath Lake	Oxnard OE W	34.213°N	119.254°W
Mirror Lake	Matilija	34.422°N	119.291°W
Upper Rose Lake	Lion Canyon	34.535°N	119.182°W

Ventura County Reservoirs

Water	Location	Latitude	Longitude
Bard Lake	Thousand Oaks	34.238°N	118.817°W
Brownstone Reservoir	Fillmore	34.415°N	118.943°W
Lake Casitas	Ventura	34.372°N	119.334°W
Lake Eleanor	Thousand Oaks	34.136°N	118.851°W
Lake Piru	Piru	34.462°N	118.750°W
Lake Sherwood	Thousand Oaks	34.140°N	118.858°W
Lion Canyon Reservoir	Ojai	34.434°N	119.198°W
Murietta Dam	White Ledge Peak	34.499°N	119.430°W
Runkle Reservoir	Calabasas	34.244°N	118.730°W
Senior Canyon Reservoir	Ojai	34.473°N	119.194°W
Sinaloa Lake	Simi Valley West	34.257°N	118.793°W
Wood Ranch Reservoir	Thousand Oaks	34.239°N	118.817°W

The author Brian Milne scouts a promising run along the Forks of the Kern River Trail in the late summer when flows are calm.

Streamside Fly Hatches Log

A Central California angler fishing chart

When filled out, this stream chart details seasonal patterns and suggests appropriate flies for the time of year. Pencil in the fishery that correlates with the month and artificial fly that resembles the natural. If the class of fly is not listed, pencil in the pattern and fishery in the "other" column.

	Caddis	Mayflies	Terrestrials	Midges	Stoneflies	Baitfish	Other
January							
February							
March							
April							
May							
June							
July							
August							
September							
October							
November							
December							

Lake/Saltwater Fly Hatches Log

A Central California angler fishing chart

When filled out, this lake/saltwater chart details seasonal patterns and suggests appropriate flies for the time of year. Pencil in the fishery that correlates with the month and artificial fly that resembles the natural. If the class of fly is not listed, pencil in the pattern and fishery in the "other" column.

	Caddis	Mayflies	Terrestrials	Midges	Baitfish	Crustaceans	Other
January							
February							
March							
April							
May							
June							
July							
August							
September							
October							
November							
December							

Fishing Destination Log

A Central California angler fishing chart

Use these fishing charts to document your trips to fisheries throughout the seasons. Note weather conditions and tactics used in the catch—you will begin learning even more from your experience.

Date/Time:	Destination:		Conditions:
Species	**Lure/Bait/Fly**	**Size**	**Notes**
Additional Notes:			

Date/Time:	Destination:		Conditions:
Species	**Lure/Bait/Fly**	**Size**	**Notes**
Additional Notes:			

Date/Time:	Destination:		Conditions:
Species	**Lure/Bait/Fly**	**Size**	**Notes**
Additional Notes:			

Date/Time:	Destination:		Conditions:
Species	**Lure/Bait/Fly**	**Size**	**Notes**
Additional Notes:			

Date/Time:	Destination:		Conditions:
Species	**Lure/Bait/Fly**	**Size**	**Notes**
Additional Notes:			

Date/Time:	Destination:		Conditions:
Species	**Lure/Bait/Fly**	**Size**	**Notes**
Additional Notes:			

Date/Time:	Destination:		Conditions:
Species	**Lure/Bait/Fly**	**Size**	**Notes**
Additional Notes:			

Date/Time:	Destination:		Conditions:
Species	**Lure/Bait/Fly**	**Size**	**Notes**
Additional Notes:			

Date/Time:	Destination:		Conditions:
Species	**Lure/Bait/Fly**	**Size**	**Notes**
Additional Notes:			

Central California Fishing Contacts

A list of some state contacts for additional information on fishing the region

California Department of Fish and Game

Office of Communications main number:
(916) 653-6420

Commercial Fishing Information

Commercial Fish Species (831) 649-2870
Commercial Licenses (707) 944-5511
Marine Mammals (831) 649-2870

Habitat Conservation Services Information

Stream Bed Alteration (707) 944-5520
Timber Harvest (707) 944-5503
Water Quality (707) 944-5523

Regulations and Enforcement Information

Cal Tip Hotline (888) 334-2258
Groundfishing Regulations (831) 649-2801
Regulations (707) 944-5521
South Central Coast Steelhead Fishing Hotline
(831) 649-2886

Sports Fishing Information

Coastal Stream Flow Levels (707) 944-5533
Fishing Limits or Regulation (707) 944-5521
Fish Planting Schedules (707) 944-5581
Licenses (707) 944-5511
Specific Fish Species (707) 944-5598
Where to Fish in Inland Waters (707) 944-5598

A California fishing license is required when fishing most of the water located in this guide unless noted otherwise. Licenses are not needed when fishing off the public piers covered in this guide.

Central California Fishing Contacts

A list of some useful fishing contacts, marinas, and stores in the region

High Sierra/ National Forest

Barrett's Outfitters
482 Cottonwood Dr.
Bishop, CA 93514
760-872-3830
www.barrettsoutfitters.com

Bell's Sporting Goods & Hardware
Highway 395
Lee Vining, CA 93541
760-647-6406

Brock's Fly Fishing Specialists
100 N. Main St.
Bishop, CA 93514
760-872-3581
www.brocksflyfish.com

High Sierra Outfitters
130 S. Main
Lone Pine, CA 93545
(760) 876-9994 (760) 920-0842

Inyo National Forest Office
351 Pacu Ln., Suite 200
Bishop, CA 93514
(760) 873-2400

Isabella Lake
North Fork Marina,
Wofford Heights
(760) 376-1812
French Gulch Marina,
Isabella Lake
(760) 379-8774
www.co.kern.ca.us/parks/isabella.htm

Ken's Alpine Shop & Sporting Goods
258 Main St.
Bridgeport, CA 93517
760-932-7707
www.kenssport.com

Kern River Troutfitters, Flyshop and Guide Service
11301 Kernville Rd.
Kernville, CA 93238
(866) FISH-876
(760) 376-2040
www.kernriverflyfishing.com

Kittredge Sports
3218 Main St.
Mammoth Lakes, CA 93546
760-934-7566
www.kittredgesports.com

Lone Pine Sporting Goods
220 S. Main
Lone Pine, CA 93545
(760) 876-5365

Rick's Sport Center
3241 Main St.
Mammoth Lakes, CA 93546
760-934-3416

Sequoia National Forest
1839 South Newcomb St.
Porterville, CA 93257
(559) 784-1500

Shaver Lake Sports
41698 Tollhouse Rd.
Shaver Lake, CA 93664
(559) 841-2740

Sierra National Forest Office
1600 Tollhouse Rd.
Clovis, CA 93611-0532
(559) 297-0706

Southern Yosemite Mountain Guides, Inc.
621 Highland Ave.
Santa Cruz, CA 95060
800-231-4575
www.symg.com

The Troutfitter
Shell Mart Center #3
Mammoth Lakes, CA 93546
800-637-6912
www.thetroutfitter.com

The Trout Fly
Shell Mart Center #3
Mammoth Lakes, CA 93546
760-934-2517
www.thetroutfly.com

Trout Scouts of Sierra Guide Group
637 Grove St.
Bishop, CA 93514
760-872-9836
www.sierraguidegroup.com

Village Sport Shop
Yosemite Village
Yosemite Park, CA 95389
209-372-1286

Wilderness Outfitters
#2 Minaret Rd.
Mammoth Lakes, CA 93546
760-924-7335
www.mammothmountain.com/around_
mammoth/fly_fish/

Yosemite Fly Fishing
PO Box 650
El Portal, CA 95318
(209) 379-2746
www.yosemiteflyfishing.net

Los Angeles, Santa Barbara, and Ventura Counties

Angler's Den
1810 Ventura Blvd.
Camarillo, CA 93010
(805) 388-1566

The Artful Angler
3817 Santa Claus Lane
Carpinteria, CA 93013
866-787-3359
www.artfulangler.com

Capt. Hook's Sportfishing
3600 Harbor Blvd.
Oxnard, CA 93035
(805) 382-6233

Castaic Lake
32132 Castaic Lake Dr.
Castaic, CA 91384
(661) 257-4050
www.castaiclake.com

Channel Islands Sportfishing Center
4151 S. Victoria Ave.
Oxnard, CA 93035
(805) 382-1612
www.channelislandssportfishing.com

Danny's Bait & Tackle
4890 Carpinteria Ave.
Carpinteria, CA 93013
(805) 684-2711

Eric's Tackle Shop
2127 E Thompson Blvd.
Ventura, CA 93001
(805) 648-5665

Fisherman's Tackle Shop
3695 Harbor Blvd. #303
Ventura, CA 93001
(805) 642-2522

Hook Line & Sinker
4010 Calle Real Suite 5
Santa Barbara, CA 93110
(805) 687-5689

Cachuma Boat Rentals
PO Box 287
Solvang, CA 93464
(805) 688-4040

Lake Cachuma
Cachuma Lake Recreation Area
A Santa Barbara County Park
HC 59—Highway 154
Santa Barbara, CA 93105
(805) 686-5055
www.sbparks.org/DOCS/Cachuma.html

Lake Casitas
Lake Casitas Recreation Area
11311 Santa Ana Rd.
Ventura, CA 93001
(805) 649-2233
www.lakecasitas.info

Lake Casitas Marina & Boat Rentals
11311 Santa Ana Rd.
Ventura, CA 93001
(805) 649-2043

Lake Piru
4780 Piru Canyon Rd.
P.O. Box 202
Piru, CA 93040
(805) 521-1500
Marina (805) 521-1231
www.lake-piru.org

Los Padres National Forest Office
6755 Hollister Ave., Suite 150
Goleta, CA 93117
(805) 968-6640

Ojai Angler Charter Fishing Guide
1129 Maricopa PMB #131
Ojai, CA 93023
(800) 572-6230
www.ojaiangler.com

Port Hueneme Sportfishing
105 E Port Hueneme Rd.
Port Hueneme, CA 93041
(805) 488-2212
(805) 488-4715
www.porthuenemesportfishing.com

Pyramid Lake
Pyramid Lake Recreation Area
310 Cabin Dr.
Gorman, CA 93243
(661) 295-7155
(661) 248-6725
www.pyramidlakeca.com

Stardust Sportfishing
301 West Cabrillo Blvd.
Santa Barbara, CA 93101
(805) 963-3564
www.stardustsportfishing.com

Stearns Wharf Bait & Tackle
230 Stearns Wharf #B
Santa Barbara, CA 93102
(805) 965-1333

Monterey Bay, Santa Cruz, and San Jose

Camp Roberts (Nacimiento River access)
Headquarters Camp Roberts
Attn: Hunting and Fishing Program
Camp Roberts, CA 93451-5000
(805) 238-8167
www.calguard.ca.gov/cprbts/pages/huntfish.htm

Capitola Wharf—Boat Rentals
15 Municipal Wharf
Santa Cruz, CA 95060
831-462-2208
http://bonita.mbnms.nos.noaa.gov/visitor/Access/capitola.html

Central Coast Fly Fishing
7172 Carmel Valley Rd.
Carmel, CA 93923
(831) 626-6586
www.centralcoastflyfishing.com

Chris' Fishing Trips
48 Fisherman's Wharf #1
Monterey, CA 93940
(831) 375-5951
www.chrissfishing.com/newsite

Mel Cotton's Sporting Goods
1266 W. San Carlos St.
San Jose, CA 95126
408-287-5994
www.melcottons.com

Ernie's Casting Pond
4845 Soquel Dr.
Soquel, CA 95073
831-462-4665
www.ernies.com

Lake San Antonio
Main Office
74255 San Antonio Rd.
Bradley, CA 93426
Store (805) 472-2313
Marina (805) 472-2818
www.lakesanantonio.net

Mac's Bait & Tackle
902 Park Row
Salinas, CA 93901-2407
(831) 422-7951

Randy's Fishing Trips
66 Fisherman's Wharf #1
Monterey, CA 93940
(831) 372-7440
www.randysfishingtrips.com

San Jose Fly Shop
11569 Union Ave.
Los Gatos, CA 95032-3904
(408) 377-3132
www.sjflyshop.com

Santa Cruz Wharf
15 Santa Cruz Municipal Wharf
Santa Cruz, CA 95060
831-423-1739
www.santacruzwharf.com

Sea Level Flyfishing
1010 Line St.
Hollister, CA 95023
510-908-1809
www.sealevelflyfish.com

Tom's Sportfishing
PO Box 647
Moss Landing, CA 95039
(831) 633-2564
www.tomssportfishing.com

San Luis Obispo County

Bob's Tackle Too
502-A Grand Ave.
Grover Beach, CA 93433
(805) 481-2215
www.centralcoast.com/bob'stackletoo

Four Seasons Outfitters
432 South Higuera St.
San Luis Obispo, CA 93401
(805) 544-5171

Hole in the Wall Fly Shop
The Creamery, Suite 115
570 Higuera St.
San Luis Obispo, CA 93401
(805) 595-3359
www.holeinthewallflyshop.com

Lopez Lake Marina and Store
6820 Lopez Dr.
Arroyo Grande, CA 93420
(805) 489-1006
lopezlakemarina.com

Nacimiento Lake
Lake Nacimiento Resort
10625 Nacimiento Lake Dr.
Bradley, CA 93426
(805) 238-3256
Marina (805) 238-1056
www.nacimientoresort.com

Patriot Sportfishing
Port San Luis Harbor—
Harford Pier
Avila Beach, CA 93424
(805) 595-7200
www.patriotsportfishing.com

Port Side Marine
Port San Luis Harbor
Avila Beach, CA 93424
(805) 595-7214
Fishing Report (805) 595-2803

Rinconada General Store
4995 Santa Margarita Lake Rd.
Santa Margarita, CA 93453
(805) 438-5479

Santa Margarita Lake
Main Office
4695 Santa Margarita Lake Rd.
Santa Margarita, CA 93453
Office (805) 788-2397
Marina (805) 438-1522
www.slocountyparks.com/activities/santa_
margarita.htm

Tackle Warehouse
745 Buckley Road
San Luis Obispo, CA, 93401
(800) 300-4916
www.tacklewarehouse.com

Virg's Landing
1215 Embarcadero
Morro Bay, CA 93442
(805) 772-1222
www.virgs.com

Valley Region

Herb Bauer Sporting Goods
6264 N. Blackstone Ave.
Fresno, CA 93710
559-435-8600
www.herbbauersportinggoods.com

Bill's Bait Tackle & Snacks
4012 W. Whitesbridge Ave.
Fresno, CA 93706-9043
(559) 485-1670

Bob's Bait Bucket
2131 S. Chester
Bakersfield, CA 93304
(661) 833-8657
www.bobsbaitbucket.com

E. Crosby Tobacco/Outfitters
2625 Coffee Rd. Suite T
Modesto, CA 95355
209-529-6200

Kern River Bait
8011 Niles St.
Bakersfield, CA 93306
(661) 366-7866

Buz Buszek Fly Shop
110 W. Main St. #D
Visalia, California 93291
(559) 734-1151

Buz's Fly Shop Too
1220 Oak St. Suite D
Bakersfield, CA 93304
(661) 395-0032

California Bait & Tackle
4516 E Belmont Ave.
Fresno, CA 93702-2406
(559) 454-1155

Sierra Anglers Fly Shop
700 McHenry Ave.
Modesto, CA 95350
209-572-2212
www.sierraanglers.com

Valley Sporting Goods
1700 McHenry Ave. #D-50
Modesto, CA 95350
209-523-5681
www.valleysg.com

Find Your Way with These No Nonsense Guides

Fly Fishing Arizona
Glenn Tinnin
Desert, forest, lava fields, red rocks and canyons. Here is where to go and how to fish 32 cold water and warm water streams, lakes, and reservoirs in Arizona. Newly revised.
ISBN 1-892469-02-2 .... $18.95

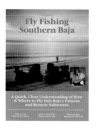

Fly Fishing Southern Baja
Gary Graham
With this book you can fly to Baja, rent a car and go out on your own to find exciting saltwater fly fishing! Mexico's Baja Peninsula is now one of the premier destinations for saltwater fly anglers. Newly revised.
ISBN 1-892469-00-6 .... $18.95

Fly Fishing California
Ken Hanley
Ken Hanley's vast experience fly fishing in California gives you a clear understanding of the best places to fish across the state of California—from the Baja coast to the northern wilderness. The redesigned and expanded version of Hanley's popular *Guide to Fly Fishing in Northern California*.
ISBN-10 1-892469-10-3 .... $28.95
ISBN-13 978-1-892469-10-6

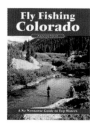

Fly Fishing Colorado
Jackson Streit
Your experienced guide gives you the quick, clear understanding of the essential information you'll need to fly fish Colorado's most outstanding waters. Use this book to plan your Colorado fly fishing trip, and take this guide along for ready reference. This popular guide has been updated, redesigned and is in its third printing. Full color.
ISBN 1-892469-13-8 .... $19.95

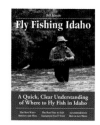

Fly Fishing Idaho
Bill Mason
The Henry's Fork, Salmon, Snake and Silver Creek plus 24 other waters. Bill Mason shares his 30 plus years of Idaho fly fishing. Newly revised.
ISBN 1-892469-17-0 .... $18.95

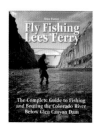

Fly Fishing Lees Ferry
Dave Foster
This guide provides a clear understanding of the complex and fascinating 15 miles of river that can provide fly anglers 40-fish days. Detailed maps direct fly and spin fishing access. Learn about history, boating, and geology, Indispensable for the angler and intrepid visitor to the Marble Canyon. Newly revised.
ISBN 1-892469-15-4 .... $18.95

Fly Fishing Magdalena Bay
Gary Graham
Guide and excursion leader Gary Graham (*Baja On The Fly*) lays out the truth about fly fishing for snook in mangroves, and off-shore marlin. Photos, illustrations, maps, and travel information, this is "the Bible" for this unique region.
ISBN 1-892469-08-1 .... $24.95

Seasons of the Metolius
John Judy
This book describes how a beautiful riparian environment both changes and stays the same over the years. This look at nature comes from a man who makes his living working in nature and chronicles his 30 years of study, writing and fly fishing his beloved home water, the crystal clear Metolius River in central Oregon.
ISBN 1-892469-11-1 .... $20.95

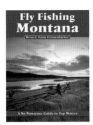

Fly Fishing Montana
Brian & Jenny Grossenbacher

Explore Montana—a fly angler's mecca—as Brian and Jenny Grossenbacher guide you through their beautiful home state. You'll get the information you need to fly fish Montana's outstanding waters. (2007).
ISBN-10 1-892469-14-6 .... $28.95
ISBN-13 978-1-892469-14-4

Fly Fishing Nevada
Dave Stanley

The Truckee, Walker, Carson, Eagle, Davis, Ruby, mountain lakes and more. Mr. Stanley is recognized nationwide as the most knowledgeable fly fisher and outdoorsman in the state of Nevada. He owns and operates the Reno Fly Shop and Truckee River Outfitters in Truckee, California. Newly revised.
ISBN 0-9637256-2-9 .... $18.95

Fly Fishing New Mexico
Taylor Streit

Since 1970, Mr. Streit has been New Mexico's foremost fly fishing authority and professional guide. He owned the Taos Fly Shop for ten years and managed a bone fishing lodge in the Bahamas. Taylor makes winter fly fishing pilgrimages to Argentina where he escorts fly fishers and explorers. Newly revised.
ISBN 1-892469-04-9 .... $18.95

Fly Fishing Central & Southeastern Oregon
Harry Teel

New waters, maps, hatch charts and illustrations. The best fly fishing in this popular region. Full color.
ISBN 1-892469-09-X $19.95

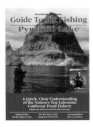

Fly Fishing Pyramid Lake
Terry Barron

The Gem of the Desert is full of huge Lahontan Cutthroat trout. Terry has recorded everything you need to fly fish the most outstanding trophy cutthroat fishery in the U.S. Where else can you get tired of catching 18–25" trout?
ISBN 0-9637256-3-7 .... $15.95

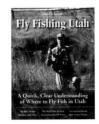

Fly Fishing Utah
Steve Schmidt

Utah yields extraordinary, uncrowded and little known fishing. Steve Schmidt, outfitter and owner of Western Rivers Fly Shop in Salt Lake City has explored these waters for over 28 years. Covers mountain streams and lakes, tailwaters, and reservoirs. Newly revised.
ISBN 0-9637256-8-8 .... $19.95

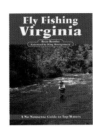

Fly Fishing Virginia
Beau Beasley

From urban streams to the Shenandoah National Park, Beau Beasley shows you where to fly fish in Virginia. Detailed maps, photographs, and Beasley's wisdom guide you through the many waters in the Old Dominion. Use this book to plan your next trip and then take it along with you! Full color.
ISBN-10 1-892469-16-2 ...... $28.95
ISBN-13 978-1-892469-16-8

Business Traveler's Guide To Fly Fishing in the Western States
Bob Zeller

A seasoned road warrior reveals where one can fly fish within a two-hour drive of every major airport in thirteen western states. Don't miss another day fishing!
ISBN 1-892469-01-4 .... $18.95

A Woman's Guide To Fly Fishing Favorite Waters
Yvonne Graham

Forty-five of the top women fly fishing experts reveal their favorite waters. From spring creeks in the East, trout waters in the Rockies to exciting Baja: all from the female perspective.
ISBN 1-892469-03-0 .... $19.95

Fly Fishing Knots

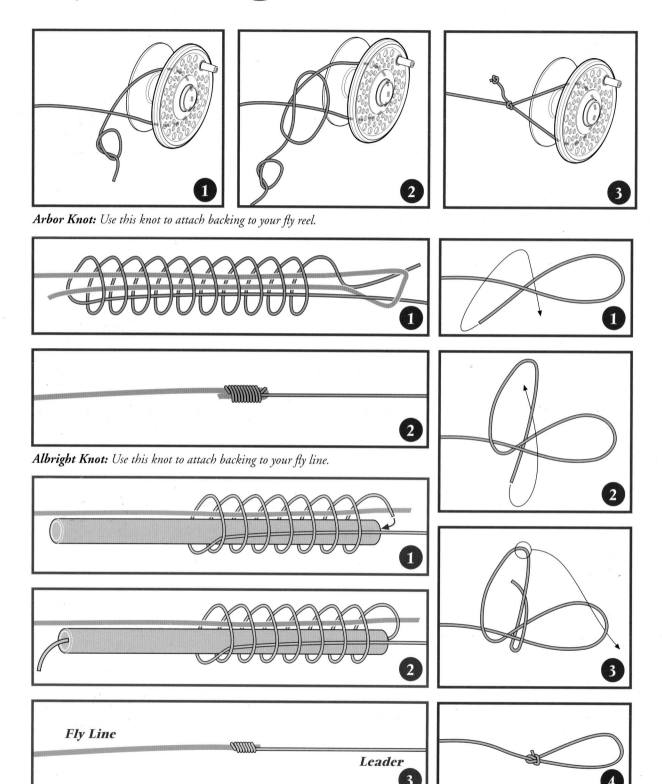

Arbor Knot: Use this knot to attach backing to your fly reel.

Albright Knot: Use this knot to attach backing to your fly line.

Fly Line

Leader

Nail Knot: Use a nail, needle or a tube to tie this knot, which connects the forward end of the fly line to the butt end of the leader. Follow this with a Perfection Loop and you've got a permanent end loop that allows easy leader changes.

Perfection Loop: Use this knot to create a loop in the butt end of the leader for loop-to-loop connections.

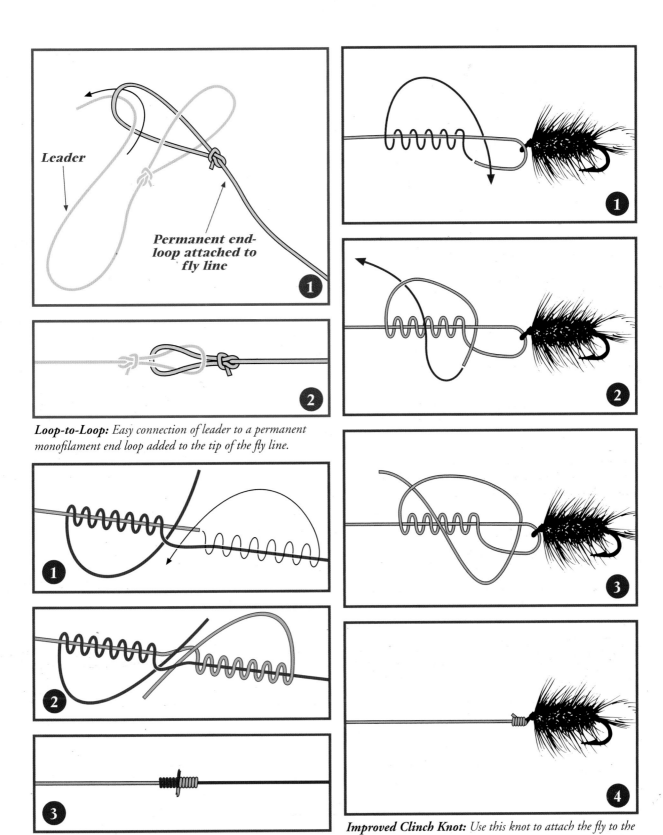

Loop-to-Loop: *Easy connection of leader to a permanent monofilament end loop added to the tip of the fly line.*

Blood Knot: *Use this knot to connect sections of leader tippet material. Hard to tie, but worth the effort.*

Improved Clinch Knot: *Use this knot to attach the fly to the end of the tippet. Remember to moisten the knot before pulling it up tight.*

General Fishing Knots & Rigs

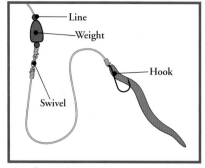

Carolina Rig

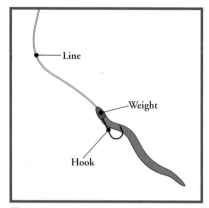

Texas Rig

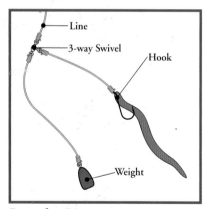

Drop-shot Rig

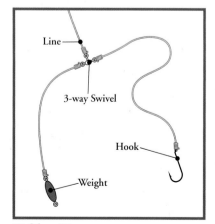

Halibut Rig

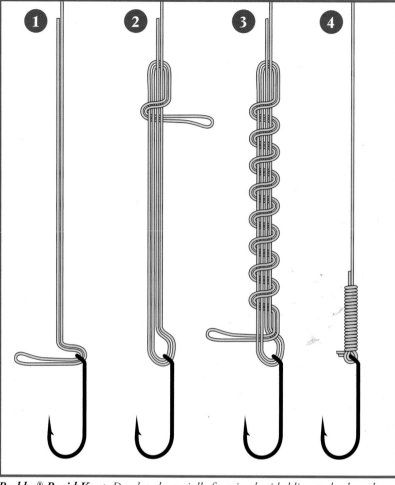

Berkley® Braid Knot: *Developed especially for tying braided lines to hooks or lures.*

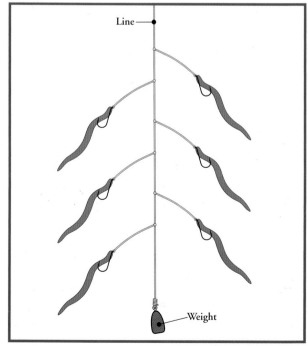

Sabiki Rig

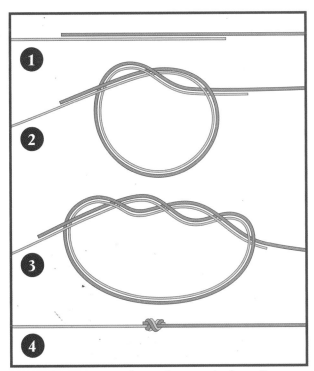

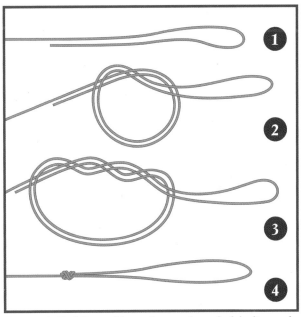

Surgeon's Knot: *Most often used in tying leaders to line, especially when diameters are different.*

Surgeon's End Loop: *Place a loop at the end of the line and tie just like the surgeon's knot to provide a loop at the end of the line or leader.*

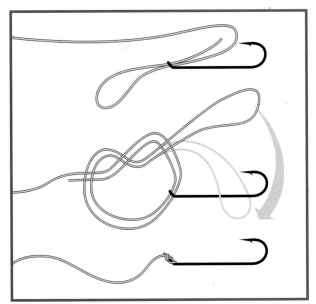

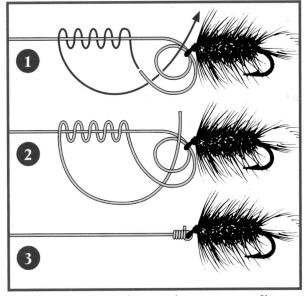

Palomar Knot: *A very strong knot to attach lures, hooks, or swivels.*

Trilene Knot: *This is a fine way of connecting monofilament line to lures, hooks, or swivels.*

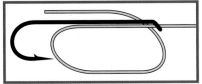
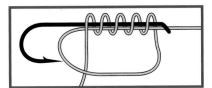

Snell Knot: *A great way to attach a bait hook to the end of the line. There are many differing instructions on how to tie a snell knot.*

Last Cast

Life is short—so get out there and start fishing!

Getting old stinks. It seems like the older we get, the busier we get. And the busier we get, the less fishing we do.

Makes you miss the days when life was simple, and we could go fishing every weekend as kids.

Those were the days. Loads of bass one weekend. Limits of rainbows the next.

Today, I'm lucky if I can get everyone together for one trip a summer, and getting all the guys on board for a weekend doesn't even happen anymore.

The author with a Santa Margarita Lake black crappie. Photo by Mark Lundberg.

Everyone's just too darn busy.

Why is this happening?

I guess you could blame Father Time. The graybeard and his trusty hourglass are nothing but trouble.

Work. Responsibilities. Dependents.

Add it all up and it equals less time on the water.

It's gotten to the point where we've turned into a bunch of old farts.

"I don't know if I can make it 'cause ..."

"I got this thing ..."

"I'm feeling kinda ..."

"Work ..."

"She ..."

And I'm the only one who's married in the bunch.

It's a shame, but there's nothing you can do about it. It's a fact of life.

We get old.

That's why fishing is so important. I truly feel the waters we fish—whether it's an ocean, lake, or a stream—are the closest thing we have to a fountain of youth.

Fishing is a great escape, and that's why I try to drop a line once a week.

Even if I don't catch a thing, which rarely happens any more because—as my wife will tell you—I fish so much I've finally learned a thing or two.

Trust me, life's short and it's important that we continue to do the things we enjoy most.

For me, that's fishing. So while getting everyone together for a fishing trip might feel like pulling teeth, I'm going to keep on doing it while we still have some teeth to pull.